HOW TO BE A
# TOP PERFORMER
IN BUSINESS
AND LIFE

# A-PLAYERS
## WITH
# INTENT

Paul J. Carroll, CFP®

A-Players With Intent

Efficient Wealth Management • 2829 Technology Forest Blvd • Suite 300 • The Woodlands, TX 77381

Phone: (281) 528-1200 • Info@EfficientWealthManagement.com • www.EfficientWealthManagement.com

ISBN 978-1-54396-148-5

# CONTENTS

*For Helen, my team, and my clients.*

# FOREWORD

In business as in life, there are those who live one day at a time and those who live with a purpose and intent for something greater, longer term.

If you're the kind of person who wants to drive your own future rather than sit as a passenger in someone else's view of the same, this book is for you.

If you're the kind of person who seeks a practical, easy-to-read, game-changing guide that will exponentially improve your likelihood of achieving your vision, this book is for you.

And if you are an "A-Player with Intent," which author Paul Carroll brilliantly describes in his introduction as one who not only already performs very well in their job, but also has the "intent" to "invest their own time in growth" and has "a growth mindset … to do what it takes to be a great leader," then this book is definitely for you.

As a coach and mentor to CEOs, business owners and executives, I spend more than a thousand hours per year in face-to-face, private, confidential sessions with these leaders. Regularly we talk about the challenges they face with their fixed-mindset staff and employees. Growth-mindset employees are the exception, while A-Players – with a growth mindset and Intent – are indeed the jewels CEOs seek, and those which they pay so dearly to retain.

So why is this? Why are these folks so rare? One reason may be the approach we have historically taken to creating leadership development. With forty previous years of senior executive positions in several Fortune Top 10 Companies, coupled with the experience of building several entrepreneurial startups, there is not much I have not seen, heard or done in leadership development – until now!

Until now, we have historically targeted A-Players with and without Intent for leadership development. We have bundled fixed- and growth-mindset folks in one target audience and then wondered why great leaders have not emerged from the process.

By first segmenting these A-Players into those "with" and those "without" Intent, and then laying out seventeen qualifiers for those "with" Intent, I believe Paul Carroll has provided us all with a seminal piece of work that serves not only as a qualifier for true emerging leaders, but also, perhaps even more important, as a disqualifier with which to identify those who might not ever benefit from the millions spent each year in leadership training and development.

I believe Paul has offered the reader the foundational bedrock for leadership success, and this book should be on the list of required reading for those intent on leadership growth.

Business schools could build a curriculum around the seventeen chapters; students could memorize the chapter titles and the quotes, and compare their "gold nugget" takeaways; and business executives could have their HR teams create 360 performance reviews around it.

The book's no-fluff approach hits its target seventeen times and gives the reader many gold nuggets in actionable building blocks to success.

For example, in its very first chapter, Paul helps the reader learn the seven tangible take-home benefits to the simple concept of daily reading. Next, he shows how the ten steps to making sure you are setting the right goals will deliver immediate benefit. Then Paul introduces the reader to the power and practicality of respectful behaviors. And throughout, he sprinkles the chapters with gold nuggets like "going from FOMO to JOMO," creating "nudge rules," and harnessing the power of developing an "aggressive patience" naturally causing A-Players with Intent to be highlighting, underlining and taking actionable notes throughout.

Paul Carroll is not just an author, but an accomplished leader, a like-minded lifelong learner and a business practitioner. In discussions with Paul, I am very impressed with his dedication to his clients and his commitment to the career growth of his, mostly millennial, employees.

Unlike many who easily complain about the problems with "this millennial generation," Paul walks his talk and patiently explains in the book's postscript about why millennials really do matter and, perhaps even more important, how we all can address their values and reap the rewards of their many unique talents.

And last, in the spirit of the 1992 blockbuster movie "A Few Good Men," this book provides the statistical evidence that shows how only a few really qualify for the elite class of being recognized as an exceptional leader – an A-Player with Intent.

For the target audience of A-players with Intent, this is a two-hour reading investment that will provide a lifetime of benefits.

May each reader read, reread and enjoy this book as much as I have and, in keeping with the guidance of Chapter 4, give copies of it generously to those you care about.

Bill LaRosa, November 2018
Master Chair, Vistage International

# INTRODUCTION – A-PLAYERS WITH INTENT

The inspiration for this book was my desire to share the values and insights I've learned as I've engaged in various endeavors and built my business. My personal mission is to inspire others to greatness, in kindness. Over the years, I have taken notes on traits and behaviors that I have shared with others and that I see consistently leading to success, both in business and in life.

Who's the audience for this book? I have two audiences in mind. The first and foremost audience is well-informed, successful leaders. Next are those A-Players who intend to do what it takes to become great leaders. This is a book for successful leaders to share with identified A-Players.

The purpose of this book is primarily to create a means to both identify and mentor future successful leaders. I differentiate between people who are A-Players *in their positions* and those true A-Players who intend to do what it takes to become well-informed, successful leaders both in their organization and in life. I intend for this book to provide a short road map for the "A-Players with Intent" to follow on their road to success.

Nothing in this book is particularly hard to do. It takes time to build the habits and disciplines, to create the behavior patterns, but there is nothing in this book that says you should work 80-hour weeks, cut moral corners, break the rules, lie, cheat, or steal. There is nothing in this book that a young professional, especially a young millennial, cannot recognize, understand, and appreciate.

I don't say it's all easy, but none of it is particularly hard to attain. My goals are to make this book concise and clear, to use multimedia as an additional resource, and to include web-based tools (more on that at the end of this introduction).

I think nomenclature is important to touch on before we get too much further. I've been asked, "What is an A-Player or B-Player? What is the difference? What is it that differentiates those who will become true leaders one day and become superstars within the organization?"

I define A-Players with Intent as those individuals who are already knocking the ball out of the park in their job, and who have an intent to grow. A-Players with Intent perform well at work, invest in growth on their own time, grow for growth's sake, and have a growth mindset. A-Players with Intent are willing to do what it takes to become great leaders. This book is written for them.

One thing that's important about intent is the desire to grow. It is my observation in life that almost everyone will tell you they want to become a better person, they want to grow, they want to develop their skills and talents. But when you measure what they're willing to do, it becomes clear most are expressing desire, not intent.

One must be willing to make changes at home, whether it is giving up screen time for reading and learning or making the best use of personal time in general. Nothing is free; none of the activities here come without a cost. But often the cost is nominal. It may be something as simple as setting aside 15 minutes in the morning or in the evening to read three pages. If individuals are not willing to put a price tag on their intent to grow, they're not A-Players with Intent. They may be A-Players in their current position, with their current skill set, who are willing to go the extra mile. However, they are missing the growth dimension that's critical to becoming a world-class leader and/or entrepreneur.

I don't say that in a moralistic fashion, because people who are A-Players in their position are great employees. I would posit that if your company is made up exclusively of this type of A- and B-Player, you're extraordinary, and very lucky. C-Players are just average. There seems to be this grade inflation mentality that a C means you're a failure. That is not true; a C is average. Most employees are B- or C-Players. The tardy ones are the D-Players. The C-Players show up on time, leave on time, and get a certain amount of work done. The B-Players are good at their job, but they're not growing. Your traditional A-Players may be growing through experience (and studies show that growth through experience tends to plateau at around four years in a position). But they're not growing with intent. They do not have a growth mindset.[1]

---

1 Gordon, Jean, et al. "Job Satisfaction, Perceived Career Plateau, and the Perception of Promotability: A Correlational Study." The Journal of International Management Studies, vol. 8, no. 1, 2013, http://www.jimsjournal.org/1%20 Jean%20Gordon.pdf.

Well-informed, successful leaders with a growth mindset are those A-Players who have the intent to do what it takes to become superstars in their organization. That's what you and I are trying to find: the A-Players with Intent, those truly growth-oriented individuals who can be groomed and developed into the next generation of superstars.

We have a website, www.APlayersIntent.com, that has downloadable resources. One is a placard I have in my office: "The Winner's Circle: Success Leaves Clues." It's a comparative inventory of traits of A-Players versus B- and C-Players. There are some other resources and tools, including a bibliography, available at http://info.efficientwealthmanagement. com/a-players-with-intent-resources.

This QR code can be recognized by new phones' cameras. Slightly older phones may need a QR code reader, downloadable from the iPhone App Store and Google Play.

# CHAPTER 1 – READ DAILY

"A person who won't read has no advantage
over one who cannot read." - Mark Twain

*A-Players with Intent read daily. B- and C-Players watch
television daily.*

There are a lot of statistics out there about how
many college graduates and students in today's world
don't read. And if you read those statistics and buy into
them, you rapidly become convinced that we're a nation
of illiterates. Well, the good news is, most of those statistics are urban legends. They're not facts. Urban legends are ideas or concepts that have taken hold in the
public consciousness but are not necessarily based in
fact. Fortunately, if you go to a site like Snopes.com, you
can discover that many urban legends are quite false.

For actual figures, the Pew Research Center found that 24% of US adults haven't read a book in the past year.[2] That's not great, but it is important to remember that A-Players are by no means average. And no part of the study indicated that those who hadn't read in the past year would never read another book for the rest of their lives, as is often claimed. More relevant, studies do show that the likelihood of reading increases both with age and with education level. Of course, that makes sense. Those who are less intelligent, less educated, or less interested (and certainly less interesting) tend to read less.

One of the mantras I've picked up is this: If you read just 12 pages a day, it'd be amazing how much you'd read over time. This equals a book a month, on average. Originally, I thought this was such a low bar that pretty much everyone I mentioned it to would do it. But I've found that most people just don't, which means the bar's not low enough. Though I stand by the recommendation of 12 pages a day, if you're just trying to embed the reading ritual into your life, start at three pages a day if 12 seems daunting.

Some people will excuse themselves like this: "Well, I can't read. I have vision problems." Or, "I have an auditory brain." To which I say: If you have physical challenges, then audiobooks work great. One of the tools I like to share is Blinkist. Blinkist is a smartphone app that provides audio and textual business book summaries. Most of the summaries can be read or listened to during a 20-minute workout.

---

2 Perrin, Andrew. "Who doesn't read books in America?" *Pew Research Center*. 23 March 2018, *http://www.pewresearch.org/fact-tank/2018/03/23/who-doesnt-read-books-in-america/*. Accessed 12 Oct. 2018.

Something that's often pointed out is that just because you don't read a book doesn't mean you don't read. I read the *Economist* every week on my iPhone. Though not a book, it's a great resource. However, and not to discount the value of good magazines, there are unique reasons for and benefits to reading actual books. I'll expand on those later.

As I said in the introduction, being an A-Player with Intent means having an intent to grow, and the intent to grow is very easily identified. If someone is not reading three pages a day, he or she does not have the curiosity or the true, abiding passion for growth, and will plateau.

> "Not all readers are leaders, but all lead-
> ers are readers." – Harry S. Truman

What are the leadership benefits of reading, and why do I feel so strongly about this? It's about more than just my personal experience of creating the formula for a successful business through reading. There's an enormous body of research on the professional and personal benefits of reading, referenced in the bibliography and associated website for those who are interested.

## 7 Leadership Benefits of Reading

### 1. Reading improves your intelligence.[3]

Research shows that reading doesn't just help with fluid intelligence. One 2009 study of 72 individuals showed that reading creates new white matter in the brain, which improves system-wide communication.[4] Conversely, TV negatively affects children's brain development, which continues through about the age of 25.[5]

If you're an A-Player with Intent, clearly there's an advantage to increasing the white matter in your brain.

### 2. Reading leads to innovation and insight.

Almost everything I know about the business I run, I got out of a book. I've read hundreds, if not thousands, of books on how to build a world-class wealth management practice with world-class service and extraordinary talent. My insights did not come out of thin air.

---

3 Coleman, John. "For Those Who Want to Lead, Read." Harvard Business Review. 15 Aug. 2012, https://hbr.org/2012/08/for-those-who-want-to-lead-rea. Accessed 12 Oct. 2018.
4 Carnegie Mellon University. "Dec. 9: Carnegie Mellon Scientists Discover First Evidence of Brain Rewiring in Children." Formative vs Summative Assessment - Eberly Center - Carnegie Mellon University, 9AD, www.cmu.edu/news/archive/2009/December/dec9_brainrewiringevidence.shtml.
5 Wallis, Lucy. "Is 25 the new cut-off point for adulthood?" BBC News. 23 Sept. 2013, https://www.bbc.com/news/magazine-24173194. Accessed 12 Oct. 2018.

## 3. Reading improves abstract reasoning skills.

Coupled with directed development of thinking skills (discussed in chapter 17), this can be a great asset.

## 4. Reading is the quickest, most efficient way to acquire and assimilate new information.

A good example is when I elected to get back into aviation. I had been flying for 30-plus years, and I decided to get back into flying after an 18-month hiatus. I went online and found some interesting YouTube videos. After a while, I realized that I needed to buy a few relevant books. I can absorb 10 times more information from a book in a given amount of time than I can from a video. Now, that is because I've developed the skill of reading, which brings us to an important sidebar. Reading is a skill. If reading is not the most efficient learning resource available to you, then you may need to hone your reading skills by reading more. This is not to say that auditory or tactile learning is not of great value – only that reading is a skill that can be polished by all.

## 5. Reading increases verbal intelligence, vocabulary.

This is an important component of crystallized intelligence, the potpourri of knowledge that fills your brain.[6]

---

6 Hurley, Dan. "Can Reading Make You Smarter?" The Guardian, Guardian News and Media, 23 Jan. 2014, www.theguardian.com/books/2014/jan/23/can-reading-make-you-smarter.

## 6. Reading creates heightened emotional intelligence, leading to pay raises and promotions for leaders who possess these qualities.[7]

I want to add a caveat. While I was doing research on this, one of the things that I got out of this is that if you're reading a business book, for example, that's not the kind of reading that improves empathy. The reading material that improves empathy includes narratives or stories, such as are found in fiction.[8] That's fantastic news for those who do not want to read only business or technical books. Reading a great novel will improve your empathy and understanding of social cues in a way that a television program cannot. Improved empathy allows a leader to better work with and understand others – traits that are persuasively linked to organizational effectiveness. This naturally leads to pay raises and promotions for the leaders who possess these qualities.[9]

There's a great book that I like, a business book, called *Turn the Ship Around*. What's lovely about that book is that even though there are great leadership concepts in it, it is built around a narrative, and the insight that the author has is wonderful: People remember stories, and to attach concepts to a story gives you everything in one bag. You've

7 Coleman, John. "For Those Who Want to Lead, Read." *Harvard Business Review*. 15 Aug. 2012, *https://hbr.org/2012/08/for-those-who-want-to-lead-rea*. Accessed 12 Oct. 2018.

8 Coleman, John. "For Those Who Want to Lead, Read." *Harvard Business Review*. 15 Aug. 2012, *https://hbr.org/2012/08/for-those-who-want-to-lead-rea*. Accessed 12 Oct. 2018.

9 Kreamer, Anne. "The Business Case for Reading Novels." *Harvard Business Review*, 23 July 2014, *https://hbr.org/2012/01/the-business-case-for-reading*. Accessed 12 Oct. 2018.

got the intel gathering, but you've also got the social cues, the empathy – you've got the benefits of a narrative.

## 7. Reading improves personal effectiveness by keeping you relaxed and by improving health.[10]

I think a lot of people go home and watch TV to relax, not understanding that TV is not relaxing. It's exhausting. The discipline of going home, turning on some soft music and picking up a book that you want to read – not what I want you to read or what your boss wants you to read or what you think you should read, but just what you want to read – is a well-established method of improving personal effectiveness by keeping yourself relaxed and improving your health. And, aligned with that, reading just six minutes like that could reduce your stress by 68%.[11]

Television is not relaxing. Like coffee, it's a stimulant. When people go to bed, the blue light from the TV screen disrupts their circadian rhythm. Late-night TV causes poor sleep, and people who fall asleep with the TV on are exhausting their brain, not relaxing it.

How do you read? This sounds like a stupid question, but I believe one of the tragedies of today is that

---

10 Coleman, John. "For Those Who Want to Lead, Read." *Harvard Business Review*. 15 Aug. 2012, *https://hbr.org/2012/08/for-those-who-want-to-lead-rea*. Accessed 12 Oct. 2018.
11 "Reading 'can help reduce stress.'" *The Telegraph*. 30 March 2009, *https://www.telegraph.co.uk/news/health/news/5070874/Reading-can-help-reduce-stress.html*. Accessed 12 Oct. 2018.

parents are teaching children to read as a skill and not as a passion. It's a tragedy. I believe very strongly that this lack of passion is why young people read a lot less than they used to.

So how *do* you read? First, vary your reading. Don't just read business books or magazines. Read also what you love, whether that's novels or magazines. One of the most useful things I ever learned is the concept of having reading themes. Maybe the theme is business referrals. I keep a list of books I would like to read in the future, and I work through that list by theme. If I'm working on personal health, I'm reading different books on diet and exercise. After I feel I've gotten my knowledge built up – and taken enough notes – I move on to the next theme.

Encourage others to read. Read for fun, as an alternative to watching television or surfing the internet.

Just as A-Players with Intent read every day, B- and C-Players watch TV every day. If you struggle to identify the last time you went 48 hours without watching TV, the odds are high you're not finding time to read.

In a similar vein, we should consider the negative impact of online activities like social media - Facebook, Pinterest, all those activities where you are interacting with an algorithm designed by an attention engineer. These sites are designed to elevate your blood pressure and your heart rate so that you stick around to see the advertising. They're like a narcotic. They are using algorithms to feed you doses of dopamine. It's ironic that we've criminalized so many drugs, yet we do not criminalize social media. Clearly the impact it's had on our democracy, our society, and our young people suggests a significant potential for harm.

Another problem with the internet is the lack of curation for accuracy. There are plenty of resources out there in which the business model depends on a certain level of curation. Outside of the opinion pages, when you look at the *Wall Street Journal*, *Barron's*, the *New York Times*, *USA Today*, the *Economist*, the *Financial Times* – the higher-brow the publication, the greater the stakes for poorly curated pieces. Poor curation damages their reputation. If you want to know what's really going on, what's true, you're going to get it from a well-curated resource.

To be fair, the internet is a good resource for high-level information; it's good for raw facts. But it's not so good for knowledge and wisdom. There's no depth. It's shallow and broad, not deep and narrow. Deep and narrow – this is where books come in. The internet can be addictive; those who work in the field are called "attention engineers" for a reason.

It's sad today that teachers have taught young people that Wikipedia is not to be trusted. And they teach this because they're tired of people copying and pasting articles out of Wikipedia and using it for their homework. But I think they're missing the boat. Maybe the homework should be to go find *curated* answers to the question and copy and paste them, with proper citations, because that's the world we live in. Wikipedia is highly curated. Yes, people can put a falsehood in it. But the curation model still works. Curation means identifying disputes. It doesn't mean pulling them down so much as just pointing out differences of opinion. Curation is important because we live in a world where people not only have their own opinions, but also their own facts. One of my favorite quotes is by

Daniel Patrick Moynihan: "You are entitled to your opinion. But you are not entitled to your own facts."

In the end, when we talk about reading every day as being the number one identifying trait of a true A-Player with Intent, we're talking about someone who has *chosen* to find the time – just 10 minutes a day. Choosing to watch a screen is choosing not to do something more productive. TV, social media, the internet, all those things – they're choices, and the attention economy has made people time-poor, because when you're being manipulated by an algorithm, you are not acting out of your own free will. It's called clickbait for a reason.

A-Players with Intent take time to read.

# CHAPTER 2 – SET GOALS

"At the beginning, goal setters see future possibilities in the big picture." – Rick McDaniel

*A-Players with Intent set goals, both short- and long-term. B- and C-Players don't set goals. The research is clear: People who set written goals are more successful.*

It is important to understand that just fantasizing about goals tricks the brain into thinking you've achieved them, and so a lot of people fail with the goal-setting exercise.[12] There's a difference between setting a goal and setting a goal with a plan. There is

---

12 McGregor, Jena. "Why imagining success can make you fail." *The Washington Post*. 9 June 2011, *https://www.washingtonpost.com/blogs/post-leadership/post/ why-imagining-success-can-make-you-fail/2011/04/01/AGi0xJNH_blog.html?noredirect=on&utm_term=.e92468c969d1*. Accessed 12 Oct. 2018.

also a great deal of research on the science of setting goals. One of the things I love about the time we live in as opposed to when I was growing up is that so much of this was theory back then, whereas today so much has been validated, and in some cases debunked, by very careful, well-designed studies.

There are many studies that support writing down your goals.[13] If you write down your goals and see them every day, you are more likely to attain those goals. Writing down goals has helped me create a road map to those goals.

In 1977, after a vacation, I had written down specific goals, I created a road map, and I traveled it. I didn't know that I was doing something unique, but clearly there are statistically very few people who take the time to open a notebook and write down their goals, let alone create a road map and follow it. In 1979, I came to the United States with $200 and a toothbrush.

**How do you set goals? 10 steps to make sure you are setting effective goals.**

1. **Ask yourself, "What's my why?" "What's my legacy, my core driver?"**
   Your goals need a motivational force. Know your core motivational force, and let it be your beacon when you are off-course or losing your drive.

---

13 Murphy, Mark. "Neuroscience Explains Why You Need To Write Down Your Goals If You Actually Want To Achieve Them." *Forbes*. 15 April 2018, *https://www. forbes.com/sites/markmurphy/2018/04/15/neuroscience-explains-why-you-need- to-write-down-your-goals-if-you-actually-want-to-achieve-them/#7fea1ffb7905*. Accessed 12 Oct. 2018.

## 2. Take ownership.

This is where we come back to that key word, "intent." Intent is the secret to a growth mindset.

## 3. Pick an outcome and a process.

You need a concrete plan. This step is where most goals fail. Your outcome is the long-term goal – for example, currently my long-term goal is to lose 10 pounds. You also need intermediate goals. Those goals are not outcome goals; they're activity goals. They can be "I'm going to run 20 minutes every morning" or "I'm going to go to the gym and burn 200 calories every morning" or "I'm not going to drink anything with sugar in it."

You make a list of small, bite-size activity goals, and you hit them one at a time. You write down the skills, the process, and the methods that will be needed to attain those activity goals. Those goals need to be SMART goals. They need to be:

- Specific
- Measurable
- Achievable
- Relevant
- Time-bound

## 4. Break up the goal into baby steps.

Make these actionable goals; outline and list small process goals. Make them easy to attain. There's a lot of research that suggests if you make the goals too big, you're more likely to give up on them. Break them up into baby steps.

### 5. Write down your goals.

Write, not type. Writing triggers a part of your brain that learns, embeds information into your psyche. Now, if you want your goals in an electronic device, write them down and scan them. Scan them into OneNote or Evernote, or write them and then type them if you must. Then look at those goals daily.

### 6. Make a map or draw a picture.

This is something a lot of people don't do, and it took me a while to get this insight. Have a folder for your goal. In that folder, you might have the written breakdown, but also have a picture. Draw a time line, mind map, or some other kind of visual. The visual will stick in your mind better. People are visual; they have visual brains. Draw a picture, and in the same vein, have a vision board.

I have a vision board. When I wake up in the morning, I'm face-to-face with my vision in an impactful manner.

### 7. Identify obstacles.

Identify what can go wrong. One of the greatest tools I have for big goals, for projects, is a web-based tool called Teamwork Projects. One of the great things about Teamwork is that it has a tab for all the things that can go wrong, where you can assign the probability and impact of unexpected derailments.

### 8. Get accountability.

Top performers report to an accountability partner. This could be your spouse, your significant other, your assistant, or another professional peer. Have an accountability partner for life in general; he or she can be a great resource.

## 9. Take massive action.

Blitzkrieg is defined as intense military action designed to attain a swift victory.

Massive action implies an intense, multifront campaign of reading, preparing, planning, and action. Massive action entails commitment, effort, and intent to see the goal through to fruition. Success is not an accident.

## 10. Manage, track, and adjust.

We're going to talk about tracking a little bit in the next chapter. Without a feedback loop, it's very hard to stay on course. For example, if I set a flight plan for New York to Los Angeles, with today's software I can determine the heading, the altitude, and the estimated time of arrival. But minutes after I'm in the air, that heading will no doubt change due to the winds.

You must track your progress toward your goals and adjust your heading as needed, or you will most certainly get off track.

*Short-Term or Daily Goals*

It is important to understand the impact of daily goals. I love little field notebooks that you can get on Amazon. They're very thin, small notebooks I can carry with me every day. I think one of the things that defines a lot of A-Players is having a "hot three" or "hot five" short list of items that you must accomplish even if you do nothing else.

And then, of course, there's "the one thing." The one thing is absolutely significant. What is your one thing for the day? This is a concept taken from the book *The ONE Thing* by Gary Keller and Jay Papasan. I love this concept. What is the one thing I can do in my life that would mean the most to me in the world – something I could do to make everything else easier or unnecessary? On my daily list, I identify my one most important thing for the day.

Along with my one thing, I write down my focus for the day, which is often an area of self-improvement that I'm trying to hold on to. I also make a note about gratitude. Finally, I note the book that I'm currently reading. I want to be reminded daily of this book to ensure that my reading program stays on track.

The bottom line is quite clear. You're more likely to attain goals that are written down, and even more likely to retain those goals if you also create a plan of action.

A-Players with Intent set SMART goals.

# CHAPTER 3 –
# TRACK SUCCESSES
# AND FAILURES

"One of the greatest tragedies in life is the murder of a beautiful theory by a gang of brutal facts." - Benjamin Franklin

*A-Players with Intent track their successes and failures; B- and C-Players have low awareness of their progress in life.*

In the previous chapter, we talked about the importance of goals, the need for action plans, and the concept of tracking. Tracking your goals is, of course, important. Having SMART goals and then tracking whether you're ahead or behind on your goals is crucial.

But there's more to tracking than just tracking progress to your goals. There's also behavioral tracking. As I said in the introduction, there's nothing in this book that's particularly difficult, and the beauty, the joy, for the young professionals who are willing to do what it takes is that there's almost no competition out there. If you follow the prescription of this book, the world will beat a path to your door.

One of the most important concepts that I've learned is from *The Autobiography of Benjamin Franklin*. When I was in London as a 16-year-old working on getting the paperwork for my migration to America, I was snooping around my aunt's house. I probably had my nose where it didn't belong, and I found this book on a shelf in a closet. I must have read it a dozen times since. I love the story; it is a great narrative and a great way to teach lessons.

One of the big lessons in that book was that Benjamin Franklin had a list of behavioral traits that he graded himself on, on a daily basis. There are people who say, "I know what I want to improve on and I know how I'm doing." That is not the same as writing it down and checking "Yes" or "No" or "I did well on this."

Now, what's wonderful is that since the age of Benjamin Franklin, there's been some research on the topic of tracking personal KPIs (key performance indicators).[14] Though that's still a great methodology, what works even better is to have a list of daily questions: "Did I do my best to … on a scale of 1 to 10?" I suggest limiting yourself to five, at most 10, items to work on each day and scoring yourself.

---

14 Hamlett, Kenneth. "Importance of KPI." *Small Business - Chron.com, http:// smallbusiness.chron.com/importance-kpi-4581.html.* Accessed 12 Oct. 2018.

Let's take exercise, for example. Did I do my best to exercise? Not "Did I exercise?" but "Did I do my best on a scale of 1 to 10?" Obviously, if I got to the gym and I actually exercised, I got a 10. If I was hurting, if I was struggling, and I got to the gym and exercised for five minutes, I got a 10. If I didn't make it, I didn't get a 10. If I didn't make it, but I went for a long walk to try to make up for it, I add that to my score.

There are all sorts of metrics. Did I do my best to avoid coffee? Did I do my best to stop eating at a certain time of day or to eat five fruits and vegetables? After a time, the scores migrate up to 70 for the week; 10 times seven days. After a time of consistent success, I take the item off the list. It's embedded in my daily routine; it's part of who I am.

What we're doing is trying to create ritual habits. We're going to talk about habits in chapter 16 – the importance of creating rituals or habits as a substitute for daily discipline. One of the most important concepts out there that I wish I'd known when I was young is that discipline is a short-term salve for behavior change.

What's the difference? You brush your teeth because it's such an ingrained habit that it bothers you if you don't. Discipline requires proactive effort to engage. A well-designed ingrained habit means it takes negative effort to disengage. Habits occur without effort. Discipline requires effort and willpower.

When you're hungry, angry, lonely, or tired, your discipline will fall off a cliff. The acronym is HALT. Well, who isn't, at some points in their life, hungry, angry, lonely, or tired? Depending on discipline for behavior change is a recipe for failure. What I appreciate about the daily questions scorecard is that you're tracking your intent.

Finally, in a business context, it's important to have personal KPIs. I track how many calories I burned according to the gym equipment, what my weight is on a daily basis, and how much time I meditated. I track my intent questions and my KPIs.

As a resource, I'm going to include a downloadable copy of my daily questions and my daily tracking of KPIs on www.APlayersIntent.com.

We've discussed habits, behaviors, and discipline. But what about goals? What do we track?

Tracking goals alone will not get you to your goals, but it is important to identify those key activities and benchmarks that are essential for success. For example, in writing this book, I may have a benchmark to have the manuscript ready in 60 days. To attain that benchmark, I need to track pages generated per day – an activity measure – as a prerequisite to eventual success.

A-Players with Intent track successes and failures.

# CHAPTER 4 –
# GIVE GENEROUSLY

"Kindness in words creates confidence.
Kindness in thinking creates profoundness.
Kindness in giving creates love." - Lao Tzu

*A-Players give generously. B- and C-Players match or take.*

A lot of what I talk about in this chapter comes from some of the insights and research in a book by Adam Grant called *Give and Take*, and though I take from his ideas freely, it is with absolute attribution and credit.

*Givers*

Givers are driven by a desire to help others and create success for the group. A key trait of givers is that they give more than they get. They have an attitude of abundance. They see the world as a growing pie with enough slices for everyone. To them, giving is enlightened self-interest.

*Takers*

Adam Grant describes takers as people who see the world as a fixed and very competitive pie. They're not necessarily evil or corrupt people, but takers tend to be self-centered and focused only on what benefits they can get from others. Persistent takers are often charming and successful at first but will lose others' respect and damage their reputation, whereas givers often attain the top positions because they focus on the greater good.

*Matchers*

Between givers and takers are what are known as matchers, those who strive for equal, fair exchanges with others. This is by far the most common style of behavior. It's more tit for tat. Take care of me, and I'll take care of you.

## *Not All Givers Win – Game Theory in the Real World*

Successful givers cultivate and use their network to the benefit of others as well as themselves. Givers see potential in everyone they meet, which makes them formidable at finding and nurturing talent. Givers are only successful, however, if they can avoid burnout or being abused by takers. When Adam Grant studied givers, he found there were two groups – those who were very unsuccessful and those who were very successful – and the following traits differentiated the two. First: burnout. A lot of givers are in nurturing professions such as nursing. To avoid burnout, it's important to be able to see positive results – the good that's been done.

Second and more significant is being abused by takers. I think the concept here is that what you tolerate, you encourage. Not being walked over as a giver means having a spine. I don't mean this to be harsh, but there are some very kind people out there who don't have the ability to stand up to abusers. They will not succeed. True givers give selflessly but will draw a line at abuse. They will not permit others to take advantage of them. This is much easier said than done. At the intersection of game theory and evolutionary biology, there's a great summary of how givers who optimize their behavior and are not abused behave. The advice is: Never forget a good turn, but occasionally forgive a bad one. Sometimes a bad turn truly is an accident. And you can get locked into an unnecessary tit-for-tat cycle if someone doesn't break the cycle of bad turns – we see this in conflicts all over the world. If someone doesn't just lay down their arms occasionally, then the tit for tat never ends.

Occasionally is not the same as every time. If you lay your arms down every time, people will walk over you. Simply put, never forget a good turn, but occasionally forgive a bad one.

*The Easiest Give - Gratitude*

When I talk about giving, I also think about something that is closely related, which is giving compliments, showing gratitude. Gratitude without effort is just talk. William Arthur Ward said, "Feeling gratitude and not expressing it is like wrapping a present and not giving it." The research is clear that for every criticism you give, you need to give at least five compliments to maintain equilibrium and avoid resentment in your child, spouse, team member, or subordinate. Expressing gratitude properly takes effort. Texting "thank you" is a very different thing from writing a thank-you card. At my firm, we write thank-you cards daily. We might send out 10 a day, and people remember these thank-you notes.

A recent article in the *New York Times* talked about the importance of writing notes.[15] People who think about themselves do not realize how impactful a note of gratitude is to the recipient, and it's impactful not only because of the content, but also because of the thoughtfulness and effort that went into it. Some of the greatest disappointments in my life have occurred when I did wonderful things, great things, and expensive things for people who work for me, or for friends or family, and I heard nothing, or occasionally got an

---

15 Murphy, Heather. "You Should Actually Send That Thank You Note You've Been Meaning to Write." *The New York Times.* 20 July 2018, *https://www.nytimes.com/2018/07/20/science/thank-you-notes.html.* Accessed 12 Oct. 2018.

"Oh, that was nice." The same person who would write a "thank you for coming" note to a client would not have the sense of awareness and respect to show gratitude to his or her teammates or benefactors, and to express that gratitude in a profound way that makes it clear that it's not just good manners. The difference between gratitude and good manners is effort. A-Players with Intent give compliments generously. They know how to express gratitude.

A-Players with Intent give generously.

# CHAPTER 5 – FORGIVE

"The weak can never forgive. Forgiveness is the attribute of the strong." – Mahatma Gandhi

*A-Players with Intent forgive. B- and C-Players gunny-sack; they hold grudges.*

What does forgiveness mean? To cease to feel resentment toward those whom you perceive to have wronged you. Forgiveness is about eliminating the negativity, the hurt, by letting go of emotional baggage. Forgiveness is the central tenet of almost all religious faiths. Studies show that those who forgive are both happier and healthier than those who hold resentments.[16] To be quite candid, this is an area that I struggle with. Just because it's on my list doesn't mean I'm always good at it, but I intend to be.

Forgiveness does not mean that you condone wrongdoing. That which you tolerate, you encourage. Forgiveness does not mean that you have to forget. In many cases, it would be wise not to forget, for self-preservation.

Forgiveness lets us regain our personal power. It brings us, as we noted, back to good physical and mental health, and it helps us clear the cobwebs so that once again we can see goodness. Forgiveness is a personal choice. Often, when deciding whether to forgive, the only person who benefits or suffers is you.

A lot has been written about how to forgive. There's a lot of research out there, a lot of interesting material. I think an area for leaders to focus on is those mentees, those individuals they had targeted for leadership and growth but who just don't care enough. They care, but they don't care enough to show intent and make choices. They're not true A-Players with Intent. Most of your team are B- and C-Players. Optimally, they're A- and B-Players. A-Players, true A-Players who show intent to grow, who become leaders and superstars within your organization, are rare – probably less than 5%. In an organization with fewer than 20 people, you might not have a single true A-Player with Intent.

Self-disclosure: Learning to forgive has been a challenge for me. I've had cause for resentment, and it's been an effort for me to get past it, though I would

16 Worthington, Everett L. "The New Science of Forgiveness." *Greater Good Magazine.* 1 Sept. 2004, *https://greatergood.berkeley.edu/article/item/the_new_science_of_forgiveness*. Accessed 12 Oct. 2018.

like to think I've gotten better at it. It is important to forgive, though, because forgiveness isn't about the other person. It's about allowing ourselves to get back to growth and happiness. It frees us to live in the present. Forgiveness allows us to move on without anger or contempt or the need to seek revenge. As Confucius once said about revenge, "Before you embark on a journey of revenge, dig two graves."

A-Players with Intent forgive.

# CHAPTER 6 –
# UNDERSTAND RESPECT

"Respect for ourselves guides our morals. Respect for others guides our manners." – Lawrence Stern

"Knowledge will give you power – but character, respect." – Bruce Lee

*A-Players with Intent understand that respect is everything. B- and C-Players think respect is just being polite.*

So, what is respect? There's a lot of talk about millennials today. If there's one area where I think there is a true differentiator between millennials and generations prior, it is that they haven't been taught the subtle dimensions of respect. I don't blame them. I feel that in many cases, their parents never sat them down and explained respect in all its dimensions. In truth, mine didn't. Now, to be fair, as any parent with more than one child knows, teaching respect doesn't always mean the lesson will stick. I believe that one reason for the lack of parental guidance is that respect is all about others; the culture that both boomers and millennials have been raised in is a little less focused on others.

## Imposed Respect - Taken

I frequently, in the world of work, run into young people who have never considered or held a conversation about what respect is. I often think that respect is misunderstood as a manifestation of fear, so it is thought that to show respect is to show weakness. You respect a big person with a large stick or a weapon, but only out of fear. That is not earned respect. In Hollywood, disrespect is depicted as coming from strength. That's not what we're talking about.

Respect is the process of honoring others by exhibiting care, concern, or consideration for their needs or feelings. It is a position of strength, not weakness. To show appropriate respect is to subordinate yourself in the care and consideration of others.

## Positional Respect – Hierarchy

Respect applies not only to people but also to position. To fail to show respect for a position is to fail to show respect for various types of authority. A psychologist would call a total lack of respect for authority antisocial. To fail to show respect is to show antisocial behavior. In fact, one of the markers of sociopaths is that they show no respect. They do not comprehend respect.

From another dimension, respect is about safety. Disrespect triggers a fight-or-flight mode in the amygdala. In today's world, that may seem like an overreaction. But in our earlier years, a threat often was a threat to life.

## Earned Respect - Tribute

The next, deeper level of respect is about tribute. It's about effort. Here's a good example I like to use. I have a client who gives me a book. To show gratitude is to say thank you. To show gratitude with respect is to send a thank-you note.

To show respect is an act of tribute. It's an effort. It cost me something. When someone gives me a book, I will take the time to read it. If it's awful, irrelevant, not interesting, I may speed-read certain sections. But I will read the book enough to be able to tell the person how it ended, how it went, what's in it. That is tribute.

What effort did you show? Respect and gratitude are very similar. The failure to show gratitude with effort is a failure to show respect.

The process of honoring others by exhibiting care, consideration, or concern for their needs or feelings is respect. It is a kindness, an acknowledgment. And you must give respect to receive respect. Many young people struggle to understand respect. I struggle to respect those who choose not to make the effort to show respect through tribute.

## Ultimate Respect - Loyalty

Then there is the ultimate form of respect: loyalty. Loyalty means nothing unless it has at its heart the absolute principle of self-sacrifice. Loyalty is "I've got your back." Loyalty is allowing for the benefit of the doubt when things blow up.

I have been disappointed in the past when not shown the loyalty I expected from those I'd invested in. I share this because the failure of loyalty will result in a sense of betrayal and a perceived lack of respect. It is something that may significantly hurt your standing. As Warren Buffett likes to say, "Only when the tide goes out do you discover who's been swimming naked" - and who's got your back.

## Respectful Behaviors

Most of us, at some points in time, have engaged in disrespectful behaviors, not realizing as much until after-the-fact reflection or finding ourselves on the receiving end of said behaviors. Here is a short guide to some critical respectful behaviors.

- Show up on time. You're either early or you're late. How often are you late for a job interview? Never, right? Most of us know that tardiness is disrespectful – we're just not always good at reminding ourselves. The worst form of showing up late is showing up with fresh Starbucks in your hand. You're saying that your coffee was more important than the team that's waiting for you.

- Acknowledge communications. Acknowledgment is not an answer. Don't leave people hanging. Let them know you've got the ball.

- When someone thinks enough of you to give you a book or article, read it! Then get back to the person with feedback that proves you read it. Clearly, some material is of questionable value, but at least speed-read the highlights, show tribute, and gain respect.

- Express gratitude. Don't just feel it. Say it.

- Be a respectful host. Greet guests at the door. And walk them to the door when they leave. Life is not a come-and-go-as-you-please frat party. Show respect by engaging your guests.

- Respond; don't react. I've been guilty of reacting when I should have responded. But a cogent response is always respectful. An emotional reaction is not.

As a professional, if you want a road map to success, understand and remember the concept of respect. Understand that respect is about tribute and that the ultimate respect is selfless loyalty.

A-Players with Intent understand respect.

# CHAPTER 7 –
# TALK ABOUT IDEAS

"Great minds discuss ideas, average minds discuss events,
small minds discuss people."
Attributed to Eleanor Roosevelt.

*A-Players with Intent talk about ideas. B- and C-Players talk about people.*

One of the constant challenges with the internet today is that you'll find a great quote and do a little bit of fact-checking only to discover that Eleanor Roosevelt probably didn't say this, and certainly didn't say it first, because a slightly more verbose version of this quote was first recorded back in 1901.

Whether this is something you can change or cultivate, I'm not entirely sure. But having a desire for growth, to be an A-Player with a growth mindset, means learning, and the hunger for ideas of course leads back to the hunger for reading – the hunger for knowledge, curiosity.

*Webster's Dictionary* defines an idea as a formulated thought or opinion; whatever is known or supposed about something; the central meaning or chief end of a particular action or situation; a plan, standard, or transcendent entity; an entity (such as a thought, concept, sensation, or image) actually or potentially present in one's consciousness; an indefinite or unformed conception.

Ideas can be actionable, conceptual, valuable, or just interesting. An interesting and significant type of an idea is a meme (an actual meme, not the cartoonish pictures – internet memes – that represent commentary). A meme is, in this context, an idea that spreads from person to person within a culture. Memes, like genes, evolve and survive within a culture. Just as a gene has a host cell and must replicate itself to survive, a meme has a host mind. Memes tend to be very powerful and are often factually wrong. Memes may be simple or complex. They are defined by their intangible nature. They may be based in truth, or not. But the recognition that an idea is a meme is very important to the contextual understanding of an idea. Examples of complex memes include our understanding of markets, democracy, and the mother of all memes, religion. Religion, as a meme, has clearly evolved to meet the needs of its hosts (believers), regardless of the underlying validity of the concepts (not challenged or debated here).

"Those individuals who cannot intermingle the discussion of ideas, events, and people make for very dull company." - Unknown

We're human – we'll always talk about people, places, and ideas … but let ideas govern the conversational flow.

## Ideas versus Thoughts

There's a significant overlap between ideas and thoughts, yet they are not the same. Thoughts happen, randomly or otherwise. Ideas are constructs. Thoughts may lead to ideas, but ideas have a sense of deliberateness to them.

## Ideas Lead to Outcomes

Here's a personal perspective. From the germ of an idea, I formulated a plan to travel afar at 17. Subsequent ideas evolved into action in the form of my career and, most significantly, the basis of my business. Though it's not necessary for ideas to lead to action, great deeds often stem from great ideas!

## Values – an Important Subset of Ideas

When we talk about ideas, one area where I really want to do a deep dive is in the concept of values, because values are important. I speak of values separately from morals. Morals are in the eye of the beholder and the audience. One's values are not always apparent to an audience.

One of the things I observe in the world today (of course, this doesn't mean it wasn't true 100 years ago or 1,000 years ago, but I see it explicitly today) is that we talk about how young millennials are values-driven. I would say often that's not true. Not for millennials or their predecessors.

I choose to differentiate between values and "feel goods." Often, I feel that the values people espouse are feel-good-driven. What is the difference between a value and a feel-good? The difference is a cost. I feel that values without cost are feel-goods, a form of moral licensing.

What do I mean by that? If you believe strongly in a position, if you have a value, and to defend that position will cost you money, time, effort, popularity, or possibly even friendships, and you do not stand up for what is true to your value – I'm not dictating what the value is – then it's not a value. It's a feel-good.

Only when you write a check, figuratively or literally, does the feel-good become a value. In a leadership setting, when you speak an unpleasant truth, in an appropriate fashion, at the cost of personal popularity or acceptance, or you call out your employer for misdeeds/misconduct, you've acted on your values. Not on feel-goods.

A-Players are values-driven. A-Players are very much about standing up for what's right, standing up for their team. A-Players understand the difference between a value and a feel-good. Loyalty is a value. Respect is a value. Forgiveness is a value. And these values are worth a price.

Values are just one subset or dimension of ideas. Ideas encompass a universe of constructive thought embodying history, arts, politics, leadership, science, people ... the list is endless. Ideas are of interest to the truly curious.

A-Players with Intent talk about ideas.

# CHAPTER 8 –
# SPEAK THE TRUTH

"Authenticity cannot be replicated or faked. You're either real or you're not." – Bibi Bourelly

"It takes two to speak the truth: one to speak, another to hear." – Henry David Thoreau

*A-Players with Intent are authentic. They speak the truth. B- and C-Players wear a mask and hand out participation trophies.*

All progress and growth start with telling the truth. If ever we lived in a world where the truth is under assault, we do today. To paraphrase a famous quote by Timothy Snyder, "The end of truth is the beginning of fascism."[17] We live in a deeply disturbing world where, again, the attention engineers are more focused on eyeballs than on facts. Unfortunately, the nature of the human genome is that we are alerted to shock, to fear-inducing events. Facts are not exciting; the truth rarely is. There's research that false facts propagate through Twitter three to four times as fast as truths. This raises a question: Why do people waste their time on a platform where they're being barraged by false-hoods? And, of course, the brilliant Russian hackers of the past few years understand that the trick isn't to convince someone of the falsehood – it's to sow seeds of doubt in the truth. And I believe that this is the first step toward losing our freedom.

A-Players with Intent are authentic and speak the truth, and they have courage in their convictions. The truth takes courage; it takes bravery. It means saying, "Hey, that's bull." In the context of an organization, telling the truth is kind. If I have an A-Player with potential and I don't sit across the table from that player and, in kindness, tell that person, "This piece of work was not up to standard" or "This behavior is not what's going to get you to the end game," then that person has no chance to grow. For leaders, having those difficult conversations is essential. When identifying A-Players with Intent, know that they are the ones who both are receptive to the truth and have learned how to protect, defend, and speak the truth.

---

17 Illing, Sean. "'Post-truth is pre-fascism': a Holocaust historian on the Trump era." *Vox.* 9 March 2017, *https://www.vox.com/conversations/2017/3/9/14838088/ donald-trump-fascism-europe-history-totalitarianism-post-truth.* Accessed 12 Oct. 2018.

Good communication skills are critical to success. Unfortunately, society has become so soft and overly sensitive that people feel they need to be passive and tentative in the way they speak to others. They tone down the truth to avoid offending someone. They are vague to avoid hurting someone's feelings. This doesn't work. To succeed personally and professionally, you need to speak clearly. You need to speak truthfully. You need to be diplomatically direct.

One thing that's become popular in the past few decades is "participation kudos." In fact, the research is quite clear that a trophy for all has two negative results. One, it doesn't make the recipients who don't deserve the reward feel better. Two, the recipients who did deserve something are disincentivized by the fact that their honor was watered down by trophies for all.[18] And I'll be quite selfishly candid: I feel this, personally, though I choose not to lose sleep over it.

The challenge many young people often face is that they've never been allowed to really fail; they've never had an opportunity to toughen up. The research is quite clear that character is forged on the anvil of adversity. To protect your child from adversity is to handicap your child's character development. Sadly, many young adults are entering the workforce without the thick skin needed to survive the vicissitudes of day-to-day living. It doesn't matter how much you want the world to be a kinder, gentler place. It's not. The best way to deal with this challenge is to start telling the truth.

The A-Players with Intent can handle the truth.

---

18 "The Harm Done by Participation Trophies." *Intercollegiate Studies Institute,* *https://home.isi.org/harm-done-participation-trophies.* Accessed 12 Oct. 2018.

For an A-Player with Intent, speaking the truth is an essential element of growth. One of my favorite quotes from Benjamin Franklin is "Never ruin an apology with an excuse." Speaking the truth is a position of strength. To say, "I am sorry. I made a mistake. I own this error. I was wrong," is to speak the truth, to own the error, and to earn respect. It is always a position of strength. A-Players don't make excuses. They just say, "I made a mistake."

As a leader, tell the truth. But tell it nicely.

A-Players with Intent speak the truth.

# CHAPTER 9 –
# BE A LIFELONG LEARNER

"Leadership and learning are indispensable to each other." – John F. Kennedy

"Live as if you were to die tomorrow. Learn as if you were to live forever." – Mahatma Gandhi

*A-Players with Intent are lifelong learners. B- and C-Players are just not that interested.*

This goes back to Harry Truman's quote from the first chapter: "Not all readers are leaders, but all leaders are readers." Lifelong learning and reading are of course deeply intertwined, though there's more to life-long learning than just reading.

In fact, one of the greatest sources of learning is failure - though I don't like to use the word "failure." One of my favorite concepts from Strategic Coach (a renowned entrepreneurial coaching program) is that of winning versus learning. A failure is only a mistake or a loss from which you did not learn.

I have learned a lot of painful lessons over the years. I'm very happy to have gained knowledge through adversity, through challenges.

"I'm still learning." – Michelangelo, age 87

The interesting thing that I have found is the more I learn, the more I realize how much I don't know. In fact, often I find myself thinking, "Oh my goodness. I have so much I need to read, so much I need to study." I believe I have significant depth and breadth of knowledge on a great number of topics, and that has left me with an even greater hunger for more knowledge, more under-standing of how the world works.

For example, we recently switched the Client Resource Management system in my company. It was important that I study in advance of the implementa-tion to keep from falling behind. That is a growth mind-set. True A-Players, your A-Players with Intent, will have a hunger to learn and the resilience to learn from their mistakes.

"The capacity to learn is a gift, the ability to learn is a skill, and the willingness to learn is a choice." – Brian Herbert

The capacity to grow is a learned skill. I think one of the sad things about most countries' education systems – I won't pick on the United States – is that while they're busy teaching people information, they're not spending that much time on teaching people the skills that enable and facilitate learning. Those skills include reading skills, study skills, time management skills, and organizational skills.

I always return to the concept of choice, intent. A-Players with Intent have a burning desire to learn. They intend to do whatever it takes to grow.

> "Learning is not a product of schooling, but the life-long attempt to acquire it." – Albert Einstein

To be a lifelong learner is to be curious. It is to want to know more. It is to be well-informed, with a growth mindset. B- and C-Players are just not interested in how the world works, in ideas. They think that they know all they need to know and are confident in their limited knowledge. It is, from the outside looking in, a supremely arrogant and ignorant position.

Interesting research in *Harvard Business Review* found that the best predictor in all seven of the leadership competencies measured is curiosity,[19] and that a strong correlation exists, across cultures, between high competence and high curiosity. They also found that executives with a high degree of curiosity were usually able, with the right development, to advance to C-suite-level roles.

---

19 Aramaki, Kentaro, et al. "From Curious to Competent." *Harvard Business Review*. 2018.

Believing strongly that one understands how the world works is negatively correlated with education and intelligence. The more you know, the more you realize you don't.

We talked about winning versus learning. To learn, one must lose first.

In the 21st century, we're seeing an economy in which the four-year traditional university education is not that well suited for many tradespeople or technical people in fields where new certifications and new technologies come along.

What is interesting about the liberal arts is that they are highly represented among successful leaders. A number of those degrees, such as economics, are teaching better critical thinking skills than the more trade-oriented degrees and are very well represented among the ranks of true leaders in organizations.

Learning is ongoing. It is incremental. Students are learning. Practice turns learned techniques into intuitive responses. A lot of people will read a process but will not rehearse the knowledge.

By way of example, there's a great book about training your voice called *Love Your Voice*, by Roger Love. It is not enough to just read the book. It is essential to actually set aside the time to rehearse, to make the commitment, to show the intent. That intent is what we'll describe, and it defines your best A-Players.

Learners develop a routine for ongoing learning. They could be reading just three pages a day. I have my daily to-do list that includes what I am learning or reading that day. My learning might not be a book; it might be a training video or something else. But every single day of my life, I am out there focused on learning some small thing. Lifelong learners are curious about the world.

> "Curiosity is one of the great secrets of happiness." – Bryant H. McGill

Look at every baby and every young child. We are born curious. I don't understand what it is that dulls people's curiosity, that short-circuits it. Is it media? Is it the attention engineers and their tools? Is it addiction, be it to dopamine, sugar, nicotine, drugs? We were wired for curiosity, which really means we were wired for happiness, showing genuine curiosity about other people.

Dale Carnegie wrote a famous book, *How to Win Friends & Influence People*. That book, in a nutshell, states that showing genuine curiosity about others is hands down the best way to strengthen relationships.[20]

> "Curiosity is one of the most permanent and certain characteristics of a vigorous intellect." – Samuel Johnson

Curiosity is a passion for lifelong learning. If your team member does not have that passion, does not have that curiosity, is not motivated to be a lifelong learner, he or she may be a great employee but not an A-Player with Intent, and will never be a superstar.

A-Players with Intent are lifelong learners.

---

20 Carnegie, Dale. *How to Win Friends & Influence People*. New York: Gallery Books, 1981.

# CHAPTER 10 –
# EMBRACE CHANGE

"Don't fear change, embrace it." – Anthony J. D'Angelo

*A-Players with Intent embrace change. B- and C-Players avoid and fear change.*

Change, for some, is a four-letter word. I don't think it's normal or natural to want to embrace change. "In embracing change, entrepreneurs ensure social and economic stability." – George Gilda.

Embracing disruption is an opportunity to cultivate resilience. Most people today fear change and disruption. They do not like uncertainty. Yet disruption, change, discomfort, and adversity are remarkable opportunities to cultivate resilience.

For a leader, embracing and managing change and helping your team navigate change are essential skills. You should look for these skills in A-Players with Intent.

By embracing change, I don't mean you need to enjoy change. Embrace disruptions as opportunities to cultivate resilience. Change is going to happen whether you want it to or not. Embracing change will give you strength and will develop your courage. Great leaders, A-Players with Intent, embrace change. Change is a constant in both business and life.

Perhaps the fear of change is the fear of loss - the loss of the familiar, of stability, maybe of relationships, and the potential for the unexpected, which could include failure.

Character is forged on the anvil of adversity. Be grateful for a challenge.

A good article in *Harvard Business Review* talks about actual leaders and how they lead and manage change.[21] One, share a compelling, clear purpose. Two, look ahead and see opportunity. Communicate that opportunity. Three, seek out that which is not working. And four, promote calculated risk-taking and experimentation within your team and especially by your A-Players. Embrace change.

A-Players with Intent embrace change.

---

21 Ready, Douglas. "4 Things Successful Change Leaders Do Well." *Harvard Business Review*. 28 Jan. 2016, *https://hbr.org/2016/01/4-things-successful-change-leaders-do-well*. Accessed 12 Oct. 2018.

# CHAPTER 11 –
# RESPECT TIME SCARCITY

"Lost time is never found again." – Benjamin Franklin

*A-Players with Intent treat their time as a scarce resource. B- and C-Players can be wasteful with their time.*

*Know Your Worth*

One trick I was very fortunate to learn by my early 30s was to take the dollar value of my time very seriously. Most people don't even know what the dollar value of their time is. If you're an hourly employee and you make $24 an hour, you know your time is worth $24 an hour. It's certainly worth what somebody else will pay for it.

If you make $100,000 a year, the math is easy: Drop three zeros, to $100; divide by two, and your time's worth about $50 an hour. Whatever your annual income is, drop three zeroes and divide by two. Always know this number. I've asked my team members to put it on their monitor or write it down somewhere. You should know this number because that's how much your time is worth – not just your time at work, but also your free time and your personal time.

Knowing this number helps give you a sense of the value of your time. It gives you the ability to evaluate. Does it make sense to do something yourself? Now, if doing something yourself meets some passionate need or desire, or is a hobby, I get it. But if your time is worth $50 an hour and you're not willing to pay $20 to have someone cut the lawn, and you're also not finding time to grow, to develop your curiosity, to read – to do one of the many things that define the intent of an A-Player – then you're really making a choice, a statement that you are not an A-Player with Intent. A true A-Player is wary of time hogs.

*Biggest Time Wasters*

Be aware of the price you're paying, because in an attention economy, it's not a fair fight. Attention is a scarce resource; we only have so much. Social media especially is programming our brains with basic ideas. If you go to YouTube or social media and start clicking on feeds that are interesting, they will get persistently more and more extreme. Extreme in politics. Extreme in behavior. Even extreme in violence.

And what are these feeds doing? They are trying to increase the degree of arousal by feeding our brains with dopamine through clickbait. It is in essence having the same effect as being addicted to pornography or gambling. Gambling is very much a dopamine feedback loop. And just as we have Gamblers Anonymous, there are already equivalent internet rehabs for Facebook and other social media.

Those who design these tools are the first to disconnect. A slew of interesting articles discuss how attention engineers, themselves, swear by tech-free time and zones.[22] They see what they're doing, and they often choose to avoid the very products that they've created. They realize the destructive influence of the addictive feedback loops. In fact, one company called Dopamine Labs had to change its name to Boundless AI due to negative press (it didn't change its behavior, though).

This is a company that sold the ability to feed customers dopamine through coding prowess and artificial intelligence. These modern development firms are certainly amoral, and it's ironic that their employees tend to be politically active against the "original sin" industries, such as big oil, tobacco, alcohol, and firearms, while working for firms that may threaten our democracy and institutions and addict some individuals to maladaptive behaviors.

---

22 Sulleyman, Aatif. "Ex-Facebook and Google Employees Are Fighting Back Against 'Harmful and Addictive' Tech Products." The Independent, Independent Digital News and Media, 6 Feb. 2018, www.independent.co.uk/life-style/gadgets-and-tech/news/facebook-addiction-google-social-media-harmful-truth-about-tech-campaign-tristan-harris-a8197686.html.

Here's a concept – it's called continuous partial attention. What we're learning is that devices like smartphones severely limit focus and are effectively lowering people's IQ. One study shows that the mere presence of a smartphone damages cognitive capacity. That is why we have a rule in my organization: I don't ever want to hear or see a text. If I hear or see a text, I'm going to be upset. Those notifications pull you out of your concentration and take, on average, approximately 23 minutes to recover from.[23]

If you're getting eight texts in an hour, you're really not paying attention. You are not in the zone. Turn the notifications off. Turn the phone facedown, and if it's important, tell your spouse or your partner to do what we did for a hundred years: Pick up the phone and call. If it's that important but you can't call, something's wrong. We survived for millennia without texts. Even the day care can pick up the phone and call.

From a time-management perspective, the problem with television is that its product is dished out in blocks of 30 minutes, 60 minutes, or more. And the producers are very good at keeping you engaged. As a result, unlike with a book or magazine, which is easier to put down, people tend to consume television content in longer time blocks than they would otherwise choose to be entertained.

There is interesting research that suggests significant online usage is a modern-day marshmallow test. The marshmallow test was done in the 1960s and 1970s to study delayed gratification in children. Those kids who were able to delay gratification were more likely

---

23 Gudith, Daniela, et al. "The Cost of Interrupted Work: More Speed and Stress." https://www.ics.uci.edu/~gmark/chi08-mark.pdf.

to measure favorably in life on metrics such as income, education, and even obesity. More recent research suggests that significant online/smartphone usage by children and teenagers may also be negatively correlated with subsequent success in life (though it should be noted that it will likely be a few decades before there's final validation of these findings).

Lest we forget, pre-internet time wasters existed and exist. These include the proverbial Chatty Cathies – individuals whose poor productivity impacts others'. Excessive and disorganized meetings. Inefficient processes and tasks. Overlong networking and client calls. Business development with inadequate research.

*Protecting Your Time*

It's a tribute to how these things have taken over our lives that people just can't deal with it. There's a term out there called FOMO: fear of missing out. I have so little respect for people who suffer from FOMO. It's a weakness to have to know what's going on; you're afraid. It's driven by the compulsion to compare. Theodore Roosevelt once said, "Comparison is the thief of joy."

> "The more social media we have, the more we think we're connecting, but we are really disconnecting from each other." – JR

All I'm saying here is that if you want to talk about the ultimate loaded gun in the house, it is the smartphone. The smartphone is so powerful in a positive fashion. I have meditation apps, communication tools for my business, and navigational tools for flying. There's nothing wrong per se with the phone; the problem is the user's behavior. The ownership of a phone comes with a responsibility for self-preservation and discipline. So, choose. An A-Player with Intent will be deliberate in how he or she spends time.

Choose to live a deliberate and conscious life. People say, "I can't stop. I need to go online to stay in touch." When you look at the average person who goes online, you see they are rarely online for less than 15 minutes. If you made a list of your 30 most valued relationships and you called one person on that list every day for 15 minutes, I guarantee you would have a deeper, higher-quality, more valuable relationship than you could ever get via text or social media. It's a choice.

You won't miss out on anything. This is not a choice of staying in touch or not staying in touch. In the end, this is all about choice and intent. We come back again to who's willing to do what it takes. A-Players with Intent turn off notifications, have tech-free days, and prioritize their tools appropriately so that they are not distracted visually or auditorily. A-Players discover JOMO: the joy of missing out.

A-Players with Intent know how to do this and find the time to be lifelong learners and grow into great leaders. They live a deliberate life, understanding the value of every minute – be it personal or professional.

A-Players with Intent respect time scarcity.

# CHAPTER 12 –
# CURATE THEIR TRIBE

"You are the average of the five people you
spend your time with." – James Altucher

*A-Players with Intent curate their tribe. B- and C-Players
don't understand that you are who you spend time with.*

Social contagion is a type of social influence, and
it refers to the tendency for certain behavior exhib-
ited by one person to be copied by others who are
either in the vicinity of the original actor or have been
exposed to media coverage describing the behavior
of the original individual. One of the best examples of
a social contagion is obesity. In an organization where
the majority of people are obese, people who enter
the organization will tend to gain weight.

What happens when an overweight person works for an organization full of healthy, slender people? That person might not ever become as slender as the rest of the group, but he or she will be less inclined to gain weight. I'm using weight as a very visible example of a social contagion. Attitudes, opinions, and beliefs are all infectious. We like to think we're masters of our minds, but the evidence is quite strong that we're not. Adopted memes – which are essentially cultural genes – evolve, and in large part they evolve based on what is considered appropriate, believable, and acceptable. To be an A-Player with Intent, it's extremely important to surround yourself with people who have more of what you want.

Some friends hold you back. Curating the tribe is something that true A-Players understand instinctively. Most people are in the business of collecting friends, collecting contacts, just being popular. A-Players are significantly more deliberate; you can tell the intent of an A-Player by the willingness to curate his or her tribe.

There's a concept called topgrading, and it's predominantly used in the context of hiring. Topgrading is defined as the practice of creating the highest-quality workforce by ensuring the talent acquisition and management processes focus on identifying, hiring, promoting, and retaining high performers, A-Players, in the organization at every salary level. Topgrading your tribe and your top five is a very active process. At my firm, we actually have Dunbar lists. We don't call them that. We call them something else, but they are lists that adopt the concept of Dunbar's number.

Dunbar is an anthropologist and evolutionary psychologist who came up with the thesis that it is pretty much impossible for the human brain to manage more than about 150 active relationships. Now, the outer circle can be a lot greater. His thoughts have been popularized by Malcolm Gladwell, and by Judy Robinett in her wonderful book *How to Be a Power Connector*. Whether this idea is true is not really debated much. The number is debated, and really, the debate just states, "Well, that depends on your brain." Some people can manage only a smaller number and some people a larger one. It also depends on your bandwidth.

I try to maintain about 150 active relationships. That is, I have a list of 150 individuals I will meet, email extensively, or call every month. They are my inner circle. I am deliberately applying Dunbar's Law to the concept of topgrading through curation of my inner circle. I have adopted a policy of topgrading not only my top 150, but also my top 50 and top five. Who are these five? Close friends, relatives, and professionals whom I hope to emulate as I seek to constantly improve myself.

What of those important and valued relationships that no longer fit into your top 150? The importance of your outer circle cannot be overstated. These individuals, in aggregate, will lead to many future friendships and new relationships. I would not advocate a cold-hearted "dismissal" from the top 150. Though these relationships are important to me, Dunbar's Law is not optional; consequently, mechanisms need to be in place to ensure you somehow touch your outer circle on a quarterly or annual basis.

What's important, though, is identifying those five who add the greatest value, who will improve you, and whom you'll always look up to. A-Players hire A-Players. B-Players hire C-Players. A-Players with Intent are not afraid to hire people who are better than they are. A-Players, though they may initially be intimidated by spending time around people who will elevate them, understand the importance of acting "as if." They can't help how they feel, but they are not afraid to act as if they are not intimidated. They understand that if they act "as if," intimidation or fear will pass. A-Players with Intent have the courage to curate their top five.

We all live in social communities. Many of our fears, such as the fear of public speaking, the fear of missing out, and the fear of being rejected, come from very, very basic instincts of survival. Two thousand years ago in the Serengeti, if you were ostracized or kicked out of your community, you were probably going to die. It's a very rational fear, even though it's not so rational in the 21st century. Despite that, the fear of rejection, the fear of being left out, is a very powerful motivator that one should at least be aware of. When topgrading, curating your tribe, the mechanics should be simple. It's very important to write down and rank the members of your curated tribe.

A-Players with Intent, once made aware of top-grading, will start doing it. What do you do about the people who are in your top five but don't belong there, or the people in your top 50? A lot of those people will be friends and relatives. You'll sit down and think, "This friend no longer shares my values, or this relative is really holding me back. They do not like seeing my success." You don't reject them; you just only have so much bandwidth to reach out. The best way to deal with this is to reach out to the 150, focus on your top five, and let benign neglect take care of the rest. If they reach out to you, you can still be polite and engage them.

Though my theme is attracting and seeking out those who will get you to the next level, benign neglect and replacement of those you've moved beyond is how you become more attractive to your inner circle and create the bandwidth.

Live an epic life, surrounded by epic people.

A-Players with Intent curate their tribe.

# CHAPTER 13 –
# SEEK MENTORSHIP
# OPPORTUNITIES

"The best way a mentor can prepare another
leader is to expose him or her to other
great people." – John C. Maxwell

"The delicate balance of mentoring someone is not
creating them in your own image, but giving them the
opportunity to create themselves." – Steven Spielberg

*A-Players with Intent actively seek mentorship opportu-
nities. B- and C-Players see mentorship as an imposition.*

When I was out of grad school, I ended up working for one of what were then the "big eight" accounting firms. Now it's more like the big three or four. I was frustrated. I didn't see the end game, where I was going, and I didn't have much mentoring.

As a result, I ended up changing my career path. I didn't know what was next. I wasn't raised in a family that talked about professional careers and how you develop them. And though I was an avid reader, this was something I just wasn't ready for. I see this frustration in young people today, and although I hear about it being a millennial trait, either I was a millennial back in the 1970s and 1980s or this is a common intergenerational issue. People were a little more inclined to stick it out back in the day, but I don't think they were any less frustrated.

When I first implemented a mentoring program, we'd just talk over lunch. With hindsight, that's little more than a social event. Over the years, we have developed structure. I experienced a lot of pushback about structured mentoring, which I didn't understand until I came to realize that these programs should have an element of voluntary participation. B- and C-Players will self-identify through nonparticipation. Let them. Not everyone's an A-Player. An A-Player with Intent is going to hunger for every edge he or she can get. He or she is going to want mentors. A great A-Player is going to seek multiple mentors, not just within an organization but also outside.

*Different Types of Mentoring Opportunities*

At our firm, we have evolved our mentorship program. Our internal mentorship program has become more structured. And we also recommend that our team members go find outside mentors. Learn different things from different people.

From a leader's point of view, what have we learned about how to mentor people? First, it's very important to create a structure, to have a framework. All of our mentoring has a built-process, methodology, or agenda. In fact, we like to have mentees prepare a feedback form to help guide the mentoring experience.

It is also important to consider the personality and unique abilities of the mentor/mentee relationship. We assign a mentor to each person. Often that mentor is not the mentee's supervisor. The process is designed for growth and need not be inhibited by relative power within the chain of command. In addition, if we're looking for a specific growth direction, we will assign a mentor with the desired unique ability to the appropriate mentee.

Finally, there are a variety of mentoring venues and experiences to be considered. Different venues and experiences create different learning opportunities and outcomes. We have periodic mentor lunches. I've heard others say they don't like the informality of lunch. But we counter this by having a specific agenda. And there's something about breaking bread that changes the tenor of a conversation.

We also have a monthly mentor-type event. We call it the Winner's Breakfast. You can have too much of a good thing, and I daresay I did in the early years, but we've gravitated to a monthly, voluntary, catered group discussion about specific topics. With the right people on board, and an effort to avoid overexposure, we've gotten a great group mentor activity up and running.

## Guidelines for a Voluntary Mentorship Program

1. **If mentees don't participate, your mentorship will be of very little value.**
   This is where the analogy of leading a horse to water kicks in. You can't force this on people. Your B- and C-Players will often resist. At the very least, a mentorship program will help them self-identify their true growth potential to you and the organization.

2. **Do not be their white knight to fix things.**
   It's not your job to fix their problems. It's a learned skill. That is, when you have an objective in mind as a mentor, it is extremely important that you use guided questions rather than directive statements to get the person where you're going, because if it's your idea, it will not be owned the same way by your team members. Again, mentors must refrain from giving all the answers. Be Socratic.

3. **Mentees must be able to take direction.**
   It's not enough just to show up. Be coachable. Lean in. Listen. Write down notes. Getting back to respect, one of the easiest ways to show respect when someone's trying to tell you something is to get a piece of paper and a pen, and take notes. I can't count how many young professionals I've

met who will sit there while I describe something, and there is no way that they can remember everything I've said, or all the bullet points, but they're not writing it down. It is a lack of respect for my time, and a lack of true intent to learn. Those people are not A-Players with Intent.

A-Players with Intent seek mentorship opportunities.

# CHAPTER 14 –
# TAKE RESPONSIBILITY

"Whatever happens, take responsibility." – Tony Robbins

*A-Players take responsibility. They hold themselves accountable. B- and C-Players blame others for their mishaps and their failures.*

One of the interesting things that I've noted is how we live in a society where we talk in the political realm about taking responsibility and being accountable for your actions. Of course, what we like to do is hold other people accountable for their actions while forgiving our own actions or those of our children. We can all be a little hypocritical.

*Standards without consequences are just suggestions.*

If you're an A-Player with Intent, hoping to be a leader one day, and you take responsibility for your actions, it's a pretty sure bet that unless you're working for the wrong leader, you're going to earn respect. It takes courage, confidence, and self-esteem to be able to say, "I messed up. This is mine. I own this mistake," especially if you're in charge of a project but it was someone under you who caused the project to fail.

To own the mistake does two things. Those beneath you respect you; you have earned their loyalty by being loyal to them. Those above you, if they are worth a damn, respect you and appreciate your leadership potential. I like people who take responsibility for their lives. Take responsibility; it's a position of power. It's a position that will earn you respect.

It's so easy to blame other people, to say, "I already know that." It looks weak when you say, "Yeah, I got it." "I understand that." "I know." "No, I didn't mean that." "I didn't say that." "I didn't do that." All those things are instinctive reactions to protect our stature and position, but they're always perceived by the leader as deflections. Usually, they're deflections to other people, and it's very hard to respect people who can't own their actions and take responsibility for their mistakes and failures.

A-Players with Intent take responsibility.

# CHAPTER 15 –
# ASK GREAT QUESTIONS

"Question everything." – Albert Einstein

*A-Players with Intent ask great questions. B-Players are reactive, not responsive.*

There's a lot of great research in *Harvard Business Review* on the importance of intelligent questioning. Intelligent questions can lead to improved understanding. In the real world and in the marketplace – the business marketplace or the social marketplace – good questions get you to yes.

## Confidence Building – Getting to Yes

People are afraid of rejection. The best way to overcome rejection is to look for it. I know that sounds crazy. There's a great video on YouTube about a person who tried to get rejected every single day.[24] One challenge he ran into was that people kept saying yes. In life, the best way to get to "yes" is to put yourself out there and risk rejection. It builds your confidence, and it teaches you that people say no for reasons that have nothing to do with you, that aren't personal. There are many reasons for a no.

If you don't ask, you don't get. You don't get the girl (or guy); you don't get the job; you don't get the higher starting salary. This is very much a gender-specific issue. Men are more likely than women to ask for a raise, a promotion, or a higher starting salary. There are many observers who believe that one of the reasons for the gender pay gap being so persistent, even in organizations that try to solve this issue, is that men are more inclined to ask. The importance of asking extends to your prospective clients: If you don't ask the right question, ask for the order, you likely won't get what you want.

When you're getting to yes, it's always good to start with another yes. Start with questions that are easy for the client, the prospect, the spouse, or whoever it is to say yes to before moving on to higher-order questions. The probability is that the momentum of positive affirmations will be maintained.

---

24 Jiang, Jia. "What I learned from 100 days of rejection." *TED.* May 2015, *https://www.ted.com/talks/jia_jiang_what_i_learned_from_100_days_of_rejection*.

*Dig Deeper – Getting to Why*

The beauty of working with millennials is that they're great at getting to why. I think millennials, in many cases, are smarter than we are. I think that a lot of what we criticize them for is basically having the sense to ask why. In our generation, we might not have asked why; we might have just shut up and accepted it. But I have a hard time telling a millennial, "Why ask why?" Let's just get to why and get past it. Let's answer the question. I would even go so far as to say that as an organization, if we can't answer "why," then maybe they've just done us a favor. Because if there is no why, let's get rid of it.

Research shows that asking a lot of questions unlocks learning and improves interpersonal bonding. It's very important, though, to favor follow-up questions to learn more about motivations and the other person's why. My recommendation is to ask three times. One of the questions we might ask is, "Money means different things to different people. What is it that's important about money to you?"

We will get a plethora of answers. Very often it's, "I want to take care of my family." There's no right answer. The B- or C-Player will move on to the next question. An A-Player with Intent is paying attention and listening. There is no better way to listen than to ask the next questions. "Why is it that you're concerned? What is the source of that concern?" Clients will answer the question. Maybe they'll say, "Well, I'm worried about … I want to make sure I don't run out of money."

The A-Player will ask a third time, "Do you … What is it … ?" It's not "What is it about running out of money?"

It's "What makes you think that's a likely proposition?" or "Are you concerned that it is likely you will run out of money?" The point of the exercise is that by asking three times, you do a deep dive into what's really going on in the individual's head and heart. Socratic questioning is extremely important. When using Socratic questioning, you need to know when to leave the questions open-ended. The thing that makes Socratic questioning so hard to do is that you've got to plan the line of questioning before you start it. Harder still, you've got to remember to do it. In scenarios and environments that are emotionally charged, the questioning can be very pointed and not open-ended. The questions then become mere statements.

Questions that are statements cause people to put up their guard. Questions that truly lead you to the right answer take a lot of skill and finesse. I wish I could say I'm good at this. But like other well-informed leaders with a growth mindset, I recognize that it's a process, and I have the intent. Get the sequence right, and consider asking tough questions first. There's also research that suggests once you've basically cut through the initial chitchat, getting to the tough questions relatively quickly will open up the client, the friend, or the employee in a more rapid fashion, to get you to the game faster. Use the right tone; work from a position of kindness. There's no need to turn this into verbal combat. Always give people an out. When people feel safe, they are more likely to continue. We always try to give our clients an out. A-Players with Intent ask great questions. When things happen that are emotionally charged, they will respond, and ideally they will respond with great questions. B- and C-Players will react. They'll react emotionally.

A-Players with Intent ask great questions.

# CHAPTER 16 –
# CONSTRUCT GREAT HABITS

"Control your own destiny, or somebody else will." - Jack Welch

*A-Players with Intent build habits to create a destiny. B-
and C-Players tend to believe that destiny is just luck.*

"Destiny" is such a charged word. It has religious
connotations. Great insights on this topic come from a
book called *Fooled by Randomness*, by Nicholas Taleb.
He's a polymath, he's a brilliant investor, and he really
gets the world. And he gets the fact that the world is
mathematically driven.[25] Life is haphazard, random.
People instinctively are wired to make sense of things

---

25 Taleb, Nicholas. *Fooled by Randomness.* New York: Random House, 2004.

that cannot be made sense of. Randomness goes against our grain, which is why people tend to create narrative explanations when sometimes there are none.

Life is random, yet we can build habits to be ready when our number comes up - ready to build a destiny.

Successful people like to believe that they're the only reason for their success. It doesn't mean you didn't work hard to succeed, or that if you hadn't worked hard, you would still have succeeded. It just means that success is the intersection of fortune and effort. The beauty, the liberating reality of randomness is that if you are not successful, and you keep learning, and you keep trying, sooner or later your number will come up. Wrapping your head around randomness is a great resource for persistence and grit.

Why am I getting into this? Because it deals with the point that destiny is luck. It is luck; it's just not all luck. It's interesting that people who have had bad fortune tend to focus on the fortune part of the equation, the luck portion. And people who have been successful tend to focus on the effort part of the equation. Both are wrong, except in extreme circumstances. This is an enabling truth, because it means we can create a destiny for ourselves. "If you create an act, you create a habit. If you create a habit, you create a character. And if you create a character, you create a destiny."

To create a destiny, you need to start with action. There's a lot of research on discipline versus habit. One of the best books I was ever given was written over a decade ago by Tony Schwartz, a business coach. It's called The Way We're Working Isn't Working. This is an exceptional book. Most of the thesis of the book is talking about energy management instead of time management, and that's an important distinction.[26] It doesn't matter how much time you've got; if you're exhausted, you're useless.

But a part of the energy management is the problem with discipline. When you're hungry, angry, lonely, or tired, your discipline tends to run out. That's why it's best not to plan on going to the gym at six o'clock in the evening. Some people are great at it, but for many it's difficult. The way around discipline is to burn a track in your brain. Burn a path where you have a habit so deeply embedded that not to do it causes discomfort.

Think of a habit as a groove in your brain – the groove that a needle follows on a record as it turns on the turntable. If you put the needle on a ridge, it will fall back into the groove. So the trick is to create the grooves. And how do you do that? By identifying the explicit habit that you seek to create, and then determining the action that must occur for a specific amount of time in order to burn that habit into your psyche. A good example: I'm trying to take better care of myself. I have created the action that when I get out of bed, I put on my gym gear and I go to the gym. The action is not that I exercise. What's important is the first step, getting the momentum.

Now, when I go to the gym, 19 times out of 20, I exercise. One time out of 20, I don't. At the least, I do a pretty poor facsimile of exercise. But the action is so crucial to the maintenance of a habit that I've gotten to the point, now, that I feel discomfort if I don't go to the gym. I have succeeded in creating a habit to replace discipline. This is just one action. The important

---

26 Schwartz, Tony. *The Way We're Working Isn't Working.* New York: Free Press, 2010.

thing is that you need to find a simple, easily attained action that has a next step. That is where you want to be. People bite off too much when they go for the "next step" first.

There's also the amount of time that it takes to burn in the habit. I think the general opinion is that 21 days straight will build a habit. There's actually quite a lot of research on the topic, and the research doesn't really support this meme, except for very easy habits. Repeating an act for about 60 to 70 days in a row is what is required to effectively burn most habits in – to create the groove in your brain.

If you're reading this, the odds are you brushed your teeth this morning, and you will brush them tonight. The odds are if you go to bed and you haven't brushed your teeth, you lick your teeth and you just feel uncomfortable. You feel the compulsion to get up and brush your teeth. That is what we're trying to replace discipline with: an innate compulsion to do that which is burned into our psyche. That is the secret to discipline. What are the disciplines that are most important? There are many, but A-Players with Intent, once they understand this, will put them on their tracking sheet, their KPIs.

I call it my 60-Day Challenge. My 60-Day Challenge right now is water for weight loss, drinking only water and zero-calorie drinks. It's a difficult one, so it is something I have established a 60-Day Challenge for. I will do it seven days a week for nine weeks. I will track it. If after three weeks I fail, I will reset the 60-Day Challenge. I may only succeed with one 60-Day Challenge in a year; I may succeed with two the next year. But each burned-in habit brings me one step closer to the destiny that I seek.

When selecting your habits, think body and soul first. This comes back to Tony Schwartz and his idea of energy management, not time management. Take care of yourself, your health, your physique, your diet, your exercise. Take care of *you* first. That will enable you to have the energy to take care of business, and the business of life. A-Players control their destiny.

A-Players with Intent construct great habits.

# CHAPTER 17 – THINK

"Very little is needed to make a happy life. It is all within yourself and your way of thinking." – Marcus Aurelius

*A-Players with Intent take time to think. B- and C-Players avoid the mind space needed for thought. They abhor silence.*

One of the most difficult things to do as an extremely busy professional is to remember the importance of mind space. When I think of mind space, I think of open time just to think. One of the tasks of a well-informed, successful leader is to be a bit of a visionary. Now, the CEO or the entrepreneur is the true visionary, and there are other leadership positions that play a more supporting role, but all leaders, to an extent, need to have creative ideas; they need to have vision.

The irony is that to have vision, you need to have mind space. One of the concepts I learned from Strategic Coach – and I can't speak highly enough of Strategic Coach for entrepreneurs – is called Free Days, where from midnight to midnight you don't touch anything related to work; you are completely separated from work. Having something that makes use of a completely different part of your brain, taking vacations, taking time away, taking time for reflection, staycations – all these things open your mind to the opportunities of the future. Get yourself out of the weeds today. It's a soft concept and a tough sell. I believe in free days and mind space so much that I have a free-day goal.

I'm embarrassed to say that my goal is 90 free days. Now, if you're thinking that there are just over 100 weekend days a year, you realize I don't take that much time off. But it's a goal I intend to keep growing. I've gotten up from 60. It's a goal that exists not because I want the time off. I love what I do, and I need the mind space to be a better leader. What I like to do when I get a chance is clear the day to make space for thought, to create a quiet and clear space with no distractions. I know some top performers – and I need to get better at this myself – who will go into a conference room in the office with a pad of paper and a pen, and have no books, no internet, no phone, nothing that can take this time away. They just engage in creative thought.

To be good at this kind of thinking, you need to cultivate several skill sets. First and foremost, learn logic. This is a teachable skill. Then learn the mental shortcuts that cause our thinking to get "muddy." Humans are tribal primates who suffer from a number of heuristics that may benefit them in the Serengeti, but certainly don't in modern life. Good thinkers are aware of these biases and try to factor them into their "thinking process." Very few are good thinkers.

The list of these heuristics is quite long; I will endeavor to spell out significant ones here.

**1. Humans are easily fooled by randomness.**
This is a subject discussed in detail by Nicholas Taleb in his book *Fooled by Randomness*. There's a human need to understand that is irresistibly folded into a narrative. "Everything happens for a reason."[27] It doesn't take much reasoning to realize this is not only patently false, but also often quite a cruel belief. Moreover, individuals tend to remember rare events with disproportionate impact than statistics would suggest. Hence, the public is far more afraid of child kidnapping than would seem reasonable, and rarely concerned about the impact of antibiotics in the food chain and the quite possible return to pre-antibiotic days when an ear infection would often kill a child.

**2. Sunk costs and the endowment effect cause people to overvalue that which they own or have invested in.**
This is why many projects persist long after they have been shut down. It is also why people tend to overvalue their assets relative to their worth in the market (the homeowner who overvalues the upgrades to his or her home, for example).[28]

---

27 Taleb, Nicholas. *Fooled by Randomness*. New York: Random House, 2004.
28 Kahneman, Daniel. *Thinking, Fast and Slow*. New York: Farrar, Straus and Giroux, 2011.

3. **Friction and resistance to change have resulted in well-designed "nudge" rules.**
In the UK, the government has a "nudge unit" whose purpose is to develop smart rules that encourage action through inaction. (Until recently, the US had this type of unit as well.) For example, making organ donation the default on a driver's license, only to be overridden if deselected, has resulted in a marked increase in organ donations in nations that have adopted this default.[29]

4. **Humans are very good at hindsight bias (remembering facts as if they knew them in advance).**
Because of this, humans are relatively awful investors. The hindsight bias leads them to believe they saw the last market change and that their insights today are therefore valid.

5. **We all fall victim to confirmation bias.**
Confirmation bias is the tendency to interpret new evidence as confirmation of one's existing beliefs or theories. There's a great deal of research on how tribal affiliation will cause a person to easily fall victim to confirmation bias. Much of this research has been renewed in the past two years. Elemental to good cognitive thinking is shedding tribal loyalties and evaluating topics on a case-by-case basis. No tribe gets it all right (or wrong).

"Silence is a source of great strength." – Lao Tzu

---

29 Kahneman, Daniel. *Thinking Fast and Slow*. New York, Farrar, Straus and Giroux, 2011.

When it's time to get some serious thinking done, many just sit and stare at the blank sheet of paper until something bubbles up. This is one approach.

Here are some concepts to inspire creative thinking:

## 1. Create mind space.
A-Players are not always inculcated in the importance of mind space. This means having the bandwidth and physical space to be alone with your own thoughts. A blank sheet helps.

## 2. Journal.
When I talk about keeping a journal, it's not a history so much as a road map, a plan, a vision. It's a dialogue with yourself, where you are, where you want to be, to discuss things that happen. We're not talking about "Dear diary, today I had three things happen." There's nothing wrong with that, especially if it's your wedding day. But a diary is an opportunity to get down on paper your thoughts, your feelings, and your fears. There's a great deal of research that suggests that this kind of journaling is very good for rumination and for dealing with false beliefs, catastrophizing, and anxiety.

## 3. Get away.
Previously discussed in detail, taking free days is a very powerful habit. Not all free days are of equal quality. Getaway days are best for truly unplugging and allowing your subconscious to work its magic. I like to take periodic breaks from work and home once a quarter if I can. I will try to go

somewhere isolated from everything that I know. I may do something, but if I do, it will be completely unrelated to work or family life, even if it's just for a day.

## 4. Finally, meditate.

It never ceases to amaze me how many top performers meditate. Never was guided meditation so easy. I use an app called Headspace. There are a number of similar apps out there. What is meditation? It is a practice in which an individual uses a technique, such as focusing the mind on an object, thought, or activity, to achieve a mentally clear and emotionally calm state. It has been shown without a doubt that it reduces anxiety and literally rewires the brain. It's absolutely fascinating science.

Anyone who's had an inspiration in the shower or while brushing their teeth can relate to how mind space permits creative thinking. Creating the bandwidth to allow your mind to do its magic is a discipline that pays great dividends.

A-Players with Intent take time to think.

# POSTSCRIPT –
# MILLENNIALS MATTER

"One of the things I admire most about millennials is they celebrate individualism, and their singularity is encouraged. To be different is to be cool, as opposed to being weird." – Sutton Foster

Millennials are taking the world by storm. One-third of the workforce are millennials. And soon they'll take the lead. About a decade ago, based on a white paper by an organization called CEG Worldwide, I made a strategic decision as I was trying to grow my company. I decided to focus on hiring and developing millennials. Established talent, frankly, did not share my values or my philosophy, as a general rule. And such individuals were often just too expensive; I couldn't afford them. But this white paper noted how there is a subgroup of millennials who are absolutely knocking the ball out of the park. They are world-class performers.

So I made it my mission to figure out how to identify and hire these great young professionals. What follow are my insights, readings, and thoughts that resulted from what was, in hindsight, an extremely successful decision.

First, who are millennials? There are a variety of definitions. Most millennials were born between 1981 and 1996 – about a 15-year window. There's a very popular YouTube video called The Millennial Question, by Simon Sinek. I'm going to draw from that a little bit, because I think there's a lot of value in it, though I don't completely agree with Simon.

Before we get into the millennial question, though, what's real and what isn't? There is evidence from personality surveys given over many generations that millennials show greater confidence and tolerance than previous generations, but also increased levels of both entitlement and narcissism. These differences are frequently overstated in my opinion, but I also believe, from my personal experience, that the evidence is borne out. Millennials exhibit elevated scores on the narcissistic personality inventory – on average, about 16% higher than scores in earlier generations.[30]

That's statistically significant, but it is not huge. It's also hard to define or explain why. This narcissism is expressed in increased self-importance and self-absorption and, sadly, in reduced generosity, gratitude, and respect. I have seen that, clearly, there are measurable differences in millennials, but it's a lot harder to

---

30 Sinek, Simon. "Millennials in the Workforce." *After Skool.* 5 Jan. 2017.

tease out why. There are suggestions that this may have less to do with the millennial generation than with the influence of social media. But breaking this out, statistically and scientifically, is very muddy, and very difficult to do. There is also a history, and a theory that goes along with it, that says early baby boomers were much more self-absorbed, though not as high-scoring on the narcissism test.

Did baby boomers not focus on their children? Were they very much hands-off? Some would say baby boomers neglected their children (and these are huge generalities). And the subsequent generation, the later baby boomers and the Gen-Xers, pretty much reacted in the opposite direction. They swore they would not raise their kids the way they were raised. So this is where we got the beginnings of the trophy generation. Everybody gets a prize; everyone gets an award. These later generations basically coddled their kids. Millennials were also – and this is not their fault – impacted by the instability of the 2000s.

The decade started with a brutal bear market in late 1999. In 2001, we had the 9/11 tragedy and subsequently the start of the longest war in American history. Then that uncertain period was followed by an extraordinary recession in 2008. A number of studies show that many millennials missed career and economic opportunities as a result. They didn't get good jobs coming out of college; it took years for the recovery to occur. And once the next cohort of graduates came out of the universities, those kids were getting jobs that the earlier cohort didn't get. Employers were passing them up. I mean, life's not fair, but a lot of millennials have been dealt a bad hand. They're not the first generation that's happened to, and certainly not the last, but at least we can acknowledge it was difficult.

Millennials are also, paradoxically, somewhat the victims of our success. The world is wealthier than it's ever been. If character is forged on the anvil of adversity, it becomes a lot more difficult to forge when one is protected from adversity. Moreover, I would posit there's a great deal we criticize millennials for that applies equally to prior generations, or to all generations. I think that first there's a perception issue. I want to go through a little thought experiment. When we talk about well-informed, successful leaders, many of whom are the readers of this book, you guys were unique individuals as kids. You may have gotten in trouble; if you're a male leader, the odds are high that you had challenges and maybe strict correction in your youth.

But the fact of the matter is that you, as a successful leader, were unusual; you were not average. You probably didn't perceive that at a young age, but as you developed, you looked at the next generation and you saw average, and said, "In my time, we weren't like that." I'd posit you're looking at the wrong group. You're looking at the middle of the bell curve when you should be looking at the top 5%. When you look at the top 5%, the differences are not that great. The millennials I have working for me uniformly come from the top 5%, and they are fantastic employees. So it's easy to forget where we stand on the bell curve of life, and that we're successful people; we weren't average. It's unfair to compare average with above average.

"American individualism has morphed into narcissism, perfectibility into entitlement, and exceptionalism
into hubris." - William Steding, diplomatic historian

Where did we go wrong? We know that millennials are measurably different – different in ways that I
would argue are overstated, though not nonexistent.

We need to first consider their environment. For
the first time, the younger generation perceives their
life will not be better than that of generations prior.
For the majority, this is in fact borne out by economic
reality. As the economy grows, the fruits of that growth
have consistently and increasingly benefited the top
20% and their offspring. In fact, a falling Gini coefficient
strongly suggests that economic mobility has fallen
considerably since the 1970s. (The Gini coefficient is a
statistical gauge of income distribution among a pop-
ulation.) It is against this backdrop that young people
are dealing with rising education and housing costs,
extraordinary student debt, and limited opportunities
for the modestly skilled. It is clear that what may have
been relatively easy for their parents has not been so
easy for them.

We next should consider failed parenting strategies. Many millennials have been told they're special,
that they can have anything they want in life. Many are
getting progressed at school, receiving credit for participation, not knowledge, often because the teachers
and the administrators don't want to deal with the parents. There are participation medals and a total lack of
accountability. They get into the working world, and
they're not preferred. In many cases, their self-image
is shattered, and it is not their fault. One of the things
that I've always tried to do is be ready to take these new

young professionals and do my best to gently mold and polish them, with a view that it will take years. In some cases, it has, and it's been a great investment.

Above-average young professionals, moving up to a higher-quality group of peers, can experience feelings of self-doubt often known as "impostor syndrome." Shawn Achor in his fabulous book *The Happiness Advantage* discusses what happens when top-tier students move into an Ivy League school and become decidedly average among their new peers.[31] The research suggests this is possibly the most difficult part of "moving up" in station and in life, and can lead to both self-doubt and depression. However, just knowing that your peers are experiencing the same can go a long way toward ameliorating impostor syndrome. I should also add that this is not unique to millennials.

The third missing piece for millennials comes from technology – Facebook and Instagram. This has resulted in the "life is amazing even though I'm depressed" phenomenon. There's a generation that's addicted to dopamine; we've talked about this. When their addictions – social media and cell phones – occur in adolescence, they affect the brain differently than in adults. I would again make the case that some of these problems are multigenerational. I can identify people in their 30s, 40s, 50s, and 60s who can't get their head out of their phone. But there is no doubt that the addiction pathways are affected very differently in adolescence and are much more likely to become permanent. As research suggests, millennials are having greater trouble forming deep, meaningful relationships. There's a

---

31 Achor, Shawn. The Happiness Advantage: The Seven Principles of Positive Psychology That Fuel Success and Performance at Work. Broadway Books, 2010.

suggestion that social media is having an impact on multiple generations as well.

Fourth, impatience. Millennials, more than any other group, have been raised with instant gratification, and they often expect near-instant promotions. I have encountered this in my own business, where the speed with which promotions were expected was completely unrealistic. Again, this is the raw material you have as an employer, as a leader, and you have no choice but to gently and firmly push back. And to teach the things that matter: job satisfaction and meaningful relationships. They take time, and they take effort. And if you do it right, the lesson is learned. I've seen that lesson learned again and again within my organization. Difficult as it may be, A-Players with Intent will develop what I like to call aggressive patience.

Finally, the corporate environment. Companies aren't helping these people deal with the challenges. I believe that whatever is true of millennials, it's certainly not their fault. It's not something they signed up for. Now, it doesn't absolve them of the responsibility to decide to overcome those challenges, and in fact many of them do a great job. If we want to be profitable, growth-oriented entities, we need to acknowledge that millennials are the workforce of the future. And whether it's right or wrong, it is incumbent on the corporate entities of America, of the world, to make it work. Because this is a global phenomenon, the business world needs to fill in the parenting/education gap, to cultivate a growth mindset and develop these young people.

Some of the things that are different about millennials are good things. Millennials in the workforce prefer a flat corporate culture, and that's great, because there's so much research that suggests a flat corporate culture is effective. Within that, we have in our organization something we call intent-based leadership, something I have always believed in.

Millennials in the workforce have an emphasis on work-life balance and social consciousness. Well, thank goodness for that. I think they come out of school with an unrealistic expectation of work-life balance, but there's nothing wrong with work-life integration. And millennials, if you don't abuse them, will rise to the challenge and work those long hours when necessary once they're dedicated and loyal to your organization. Millennials want meaningful work; so do I. Do millennials have a weaker sense of self, creating a need for constant validation? There's conflicting research on this. They have greater self-importance but weaker self-esteem and weaker self-identity. I really believe this is less generational and more about social media. However, it is something that can be developed. They are values-oriented.

An interesting manifestation of being raised during the financial crises and the so-called war on terror (as if terrorism were a new phenomenon) is that millennials are measurably risk-averse compared with recent previous generations. We see this in our firm, with successful young families investing far more conservatively than appropriate given their income potential and age.

"Above all, we want millennials to realize that they can have an impact on the world and that, in the course of empowering others, they can also empower themselves." – Nicholas Kristof

There is evidence that many of the negative perceptions of millennials have been overstated, exaggerated, and have led to unfair stereotypes, painting all millennials unfairly with the same brush. In fact, a look back at our archives suggests that many of the same criticisms were laid against the baby boomers, who retrospectively were decidedly not the greatest generation. It's that classic saying: When you point a finger at somebody, you might want to look at how many fingers you've got pointed back at yourself.

Surely, today's poisonous tribal atmosphere, both social and political, is not the fault of millennials. In fact, I would argue that they're our last best hope to figure out a way through this environment.

"Millennials are the future of our country and of our political parties, and they shouldn't be unfairly characterized or labeled. They deserve to be heard." - Dana Perino

The good news that I have found, in my organization, is that regardless of the degree of severity of these challenges, they can be overcome. We can teach the skills necessary to overcome the lack of effective parenting and the impact of an increasingly narcissistic society. To the extent that you've got an A-Player with Intent, that person will be amenable to change. That person is an A-Player if he or she has an intent to take the actions, to do what it takes to become a future great leader. The decision to focus on developing young millennial talent has been an enormous success for our organization.

"I'm very encouraged by millennials and their drive to make the world a better place." - John Mackey

The interesting thing about Gen Z, coming along behind the millennials, is that there are many who believe the pendulum is in fact swinging back. Working with anecdotal evidence, I think the parents of Gen Z saw the failed strategies of the boomers and have compensated. They don't want to raise their kids quite as coddled as the generation prior. Millennials can be very hardworking, but it's easier to tell the story of the ones who are entitled. One of the best decisions of my business has been to focus on developing young talent. There have been speed bumps along the way, but it's been a great decision.

# CONCLUSION:
# BECOMING SUCCESSFUL LEADERS

The purpose of this book, *A-Players with Intent*, has been to provide a road map for those true A-Players willing to do what it takes to be well-informed, successful business leaders.

The original list that these chapters came from was on the wall in our office and has been modified by the process of writing this book, partly to consolidate for brevity and to add relevance. Everything here is my opinion, my experience, my values.

My book should be only one of dozens, even hundreds, that a true A-Player with Intent will read over his or her life and career. I hope that it is one of those books that is filled with content that will leverage growth going forward. I hope that this provides a great road map for success for the next generation of true A-Players.

It's important to understand that it's okay not to be an A-Player with Intent. Not everyone, not all your best people, can be true A-Players with Intent. They can be A-Players in their position, but true organizational A-Players with intent to grow – those are rare. They are true diamonds in the rough, regardless of genera-tion. If that's you, then make a choice. Either decide to be happy being a great employee – loyal, dedicated, hardworking – or make a choice to develop to become that A-Player with a burning intent to focus on growth. Take the road to becoming a superstar leader within your organization.

I wish you the best of success.

Paul Carroll
December 2018

# ABOUT PAUL CARROLL

**Paul J. Carroll, CFP**®, is the principal and founder of Efficient Wealth Management, which provides consultative wealth management solutions to energy successful, well-informed leaders. Working with his multidisciplinary team of experts, Paul helps successful leaders address their biggest financial concerns: preserving their wealth, mitigating taxes, taking care of their heirs, ensuring their assets aren't unjustly taken, and managing charitable giving.

Paul uses a consultative process to gain a detailed understanding of his clients' deepest values and goals. He then employs customized recommendations designed to address each client's unique needs and goals.

Successful executives and entrepreneurs work with Paul to:

- Develop and implement a comprehensive wealth management plan to help them reach their financial dreams.

- Make smarter decisions in today's uncertain political, economic, and social environment.

- Obtain an independent second opinion from a top financial advisor in their community.

Paul is uniquely positioned to understand the needs of his clients. He is the author of a number of articles and white papers dedicated to successful leaders and their families, including "Platform for Retirement." He is a Certified Financial Planner™ with a master's degree in finance from Texas A&M University. Previously, Paul was a financial advisor with Smith Barney.

Paul is active in the local chapter of the Financial Planning Association and was awarded Houston's Top Wealth Managers Award for 2013, 2015, 2016, 2017, and 2018 by the *Houston Business Journal*. He has authored a number of articles, white papers, and video presentations addressing various advanced financial planning issues. These are available in the "Who We Are" section of www.EfficientWealthManagement.com.

# ABOUT BILL LAROSA

**Bill LaRosa** is a master chair of Vistage International. In this role for the past 8 years, he delightfully spends over 1,000 hours per year in face-to-face, private, confidential, leadership coaching sessions with nearly 100 of the nation's greatest CEOs, business owners and executives.

Prior to this, Bill held worldwide executive leadership positions at General Electric for 20 years, at IBM for 10 years, and at Silicon Graphics and Advanced Micro Devices for 3 years each.

He has lived and worked in over 2 dozen countries and has founded several technology companies, including Lead Group International. He has held senior executive roles in startups such as American Motion Systems and Global Foundries.

Bill has sat on a wide variety of governance and advisory, public and private boards, including Vitesse (NASDAQ), Lead Group International, Erinyess, STORSpeed, the Lubin School of Business, Heat Genie and Austin Classical Guitar.

Bill has a BS in electrical and electronic engineering from Manhattan College, an MBA in finance and general management from Pace University, and numerous executive development course certificates from General Electric and IBM.

Bill enjoys playing '60s acoustic and electric guitar and golf. He has 2 daughters and 2 grandchildren, and he currently resides with his wife, Mary, in the Austin hill country.

# ACKNOWLEDGMENTS

The author of any book is disproportionately credited with the effort involved in such an undertaking. The truth is, though the kernel of the idea was mine, the massive efforts of editors, proofreaders, peers, consultants, and staff played a major role in converting that idea into a readable book.

In the spirit of gratitude, it is important to me to thank all those involved, with special mention as follows:

Ken Proctor - Ken has been a friend, coach, and mentor both to me and to Efficient Wealth Management, LLC, for many years. I've worked with many businesses and business advisors. In the Houston market, Ken stands head and shoulders above the competition. Ken has helped me navigate many shoals over the years, and I consider him an integral member of my team. Ken's fingerprints can be found throughout this book.

Bill LaRosa - I met Bill as I developed our Austin market. Bill is a Vistage Master Chair. Vistage is the world's leading CEO coaching organization. Bill and I have traded notes often on best practices for small and midsize businesses. I very much appreciate his review of and input on the original manuscript.

Nathan Harness, Ph.D. - I've worked closely with Nathan, the Director of Financial Planning at Texas A&M University. He's helped identify extraordinary talent for my firm, while I've been able to provide feedback to further improve the university's outstanding financial planning department. Nathan and I have shared notes on the behaviors that will best serve his young graduates as they move into the professional world. This book has benefited from these conversations.

My team – With a special mention for Koiula Lau, my team gets the unenviable task of taking my vision and very raw script, improving them, and then selling those improvements to me. For every hour I put into this book, they have put 10 or 20. When asked what I most enjoy about my profession and business, I feel that the "right" answer is the ability to improve the lives of my clients. My belief is that by patiently grooming extraordinary young professionals to do a thorough and great job, I best serve my clients. My greatest joy comes from watching these young A-Players mature into world-class professionals. They truly are the inspiration for this book.

This is not an exclusive list by any means. Thank you to all who have added value to this process.

And if you're reading this, thank you for making it through this book. I truly hope that it added value to your personal and/or professional life.

I wish you the best of success.

Paul Carroll, CFP®